TAIRT TALK

OR

THE LANGUAGE OF KIRTON

by

KEN PEARSON

19 95

RICHARD KAY
80 SLEAFORD ROAD • BOSTON • LINCOLNSHIRE • PE21 8EU

The right of Ken Pearson to be identified as the author of this work has been asserted by him in accordance with the Copyright, Designs and Patents Act 1988.

Typeset by the publisher on an AppleMac Plus computer using Microsoft Word® and Pagemaker® applications with camera ready copy reproduced initially by means of a LaserWriter Plus laser printer.

Printed by
Woolnough Bookbinding Ltd., Express Works, Church Street, Irthlingborough, Northants. NN9 5SE

A

a – on. 'We can't go today, so we s'll have to go a Sunday instead.'

abear – endure, put up with. Usually negative: 'I can't abear that woman.'

according-lie – according. Commonly used when citing an acceptade of reference. 'London's an hundred and twelve, according-lie to the RAC map.' 'It's now five-and-twenty to five, just gone, according-lie to the [radio] pips.'

aeriated – worked up, annoyed. 'It's nothing to get aeriated about.'

afe – half.

afore – before.

agen – (rhymes with 'a fen') against; in close proximity to. 'That house is agen the sea bank.' Also, leaning on: 'The long ladder is still agen yon stack.'

air! aer! – expression of disdain, dismissal, derision. 'I got here fost, aer!'

aise! – yes, emphatically.

all ends up – totally, emphatically. 'We took a team there last year, beat 'em all ends up.'

all of a tiz-woz – in a state of mild frenzy or excitement.

all over alike – 'It makes me go all over alike' means that a responsive sensual experience has been generated, as from sucking a lemon or hearing an owl on a dark night.

all over the shop – everywhere. 'Never stops in a job long; he's wocked all over the shop.'

all over them (him) – easily winning a competitive game.

all rip – energetically, enthusiastically. 'I come past your place, see you wassing into the garden all rip.'

all that – probably more. 'Aye, it's all that' means, 'I think you may have underestimated.'

all there; not all there – the first means 'astute, clear-headed', the second, 'bordering on mental deficiency.'

ant-watter – boiling water in a kettle, carried hurriedly to the nest of the doomed ants.

any road up – anyway.

apple-cart: upset the apple-cart (and spilt all the oranges) – done something to seriously damage an otherwise satisfactory situation.

arc: the arc – a narrow line of high cloud across the sky. We used to run and tell grandad which points of the compass it was lying on, and in return got a weather forecast. It was occasionally right.

argle – argue.

arn – earn.

arse-over-breakfast-time – head over heels.

arse-uppards – inverted.

article – vessel kept under the bed in houses where the thunderbox was at the other end of the garden. Poe.

as – that. 'I just wanted to be sure as you hadn't forgot.'

ash felt – asphalt.

aspidestra – aspidistra.

ast – ask, asked. To be 'ast in church' is to have the banns read before marriage.

as was – attached to a woman's maiden name after her marriage, to identify her to a listener who might not know the married name. 'Mrs Smith – you know, Lizzie Biggadyke as was.' A girl who has married is said to have 'become an as was.'

Atkin(s), etc. – many surnames get a gratuitous 's': Mellor(s), Stead(s), Flower(s), Lyon(s).

auction, the – everywhere. 'I've nivver seen so many rabbits – they're all ower the auction!'

awming – restless, aimless bodily movement, especially to the annoyance of others. 'Will you stop awming about and get your tea!'

ax, axed – ask, asked. 'I don't know whether they're coming. I haven't axed 'em.'

ayther – either.

B

back end – late autumn and winter, generally meaning up to Christmas.

backer – tobacco.

back-hander – tip or gratuity, most likely given surreptitiously, often as a bribe.

backuds – backwards.

back up – 'He's got his back up' means that he is huffy; in a state of ill-humour.

back way – alternative route, usually by inferior roads. 'We'll go back way, miss the wost of the traffic.' Also, the rear of a house or other premises.

bad apple: 'There's a bad apple in every barrel' – said when one member of a team or group proves to be worthless or dishonest: implying that he should be ousted before it spreads.

badly – ill.

bag-hook – metal hook mounted on a wooden cross-handle, for manually dragging or lifting filled sacks.

bag-needle – large curved needle used with twine to close the mouths of filled sacks.

bag(s) – claim. 'Hey, put that down! I baggsed it!'

bairns – children of the family. Children of the school or street are kids, except that one singled out for sympathetic attention might become temporarily a bairn.

bamboozled – confused, puzzled. 'Help us to fill this form in; it's got me bamboozled.'

banker – manual worker on sea defences or waterway banks.

banty – bantam, a small domestic fowl. A banty-egg is that of the bantam, though the name is also applied jokingly to undersized eggs of other hens.

Bardney: 'Are you from Bardney?' – a reminder that a door has been left open.

bats, batty – slightly mad or eccentric.

batter – dyke-side.

batting along going briskly. 'I last see him on his bike, batting along towards Frampton.'

battle-twig – earwig. 'If you get one in your ear it'll tittle your brains till you die.'

baulk – retch.

bealing – crying; calling; wailing; especially of an animal doing so persistently. 'One o' them beast set up bealing, kep me awake while daylight.' Also, a baby's crying. Also, loud laughter. See bloor.

beating – a paid occupation for boys during school holidays. They attended a shoot and went ahead of the guns, beating the growth with sticks to put up the game. The beaters I knew all came back alive. Also, the spring-cleaning task of lambasting the dust out of a carpet hung over a clothes-line. 'Them sweepers is all right, but they don't fetch it all out like a beating.'

beck – a natural stream. A little-used term in South Linconshire, where any substantial waterway which is not a river is probably man-made and called a drain or, if small, a dyke. On the salt marshes the natural small waterways are creeks.

bed-mate – a brick in a sock, a blanket-wrapped oven shelf, a large stone, or a sand-filled tin. Hot, and despatched to bed half an hour before bed-time.

begoe, big-o – mild exclamation of surprise.

belt: 'The belt's off the boiler!' – stock facetious suggestion when a piece of apparatus unexpectedly fails in some way. On a threshing-set a frequent cause of stoppage was the flat driving belt slipping off the pulley on the steam engine.

berrying – pulling (harvesting) gooseberries. Always casual piecework. If Mam was 'in the berries' we used to go after school and pull into her basket.

bested – beaten; conquered; overcome in competitive activity. Also, having given up: 'I can't do no more, I'm bested by it.'

bet – beaten. 'Let me try again; I don't like being bet by owt.'

'Better than a slap across the belly with a wet fish' – said of an inferior but nevertheless acceptable alternative. Also used thankfully when something turns out much better than expected.

bike-store – A place in town where incoming yokels could park their bikes for threepence a time.

birch-broom – 'You look like a birch-broom in fits' – your hair is untidy.

bit – plot of land for cultivation, usually called after its owner or occupier: 'Taylor's bit;' 'Owd Cuppleditch's gel's husband's bit,' etc. Many agricultural workers rent a bit as a sideline, growing what needs attention at off-peak times in their main employment. Their produce 'tops-up' many bulk lorry-loads with lettuce, celery, radishes, or rhubarb. [Similar to an allotment although not necessarily rented from the local authority as is usually the case with allotments.]

bit dropped off – something comparatively small. Of a smallish man whose wife is generously built: 'He looks like a bit dropped off her.'

blab – let on; spill the beans; tell what would perhaps be better not told.

black dog – A person or child displaying persistent ill-temper is told: 'I see you've got the black dog on your back.'

black van – A high-spirited body behaving in a crazy, demented way might hear: 'Look out! Yon's the black van coming!' This was

supposed to be a vehicle sent round from the asylum to collect patients.

blacklng ower – blacking over. Digging or ploughing, especially grass or overgrown land; i.e. changing its colour from green to black.

blacks – wisps of light soot floating in the air from a fire or lamp.

bleb – bubble or tumescent dome; tar-bubble on the road in summer; ominous swelling on the side of a bike tyre; ditto on a young male neck.

blind 'un – plant which fails to produce an expected flower.

bloomers – ladies' knickers, especially voluminous ones.

bloor, bloort – call out, usually of animals. 'Somebody had a beast bloorting till well after midnight.'

blow – common, very mild expletive; permitted even in houses where 'damn' is wicked.

blown – (of a bird's egg) emptied by pricking and blowing.

blubber – weep audibly.

blurt – pour out rapidly and fiercely, as water or smoke. 'It med an hole in the butt, and the watter was blurting out all ower.'

bluther – talk incoherently or nonsensically. 'What's he bluthering about now?'

boats – boots, especially those noticeably larger than one's own.

bobble – ball of loosely fastened wool to decorate a hat, etc.

bod – bird.

bodged, bodged up – mended inexpertly; made to work pending permanent repair.

bod-scarrer – bird-scarer, rhyming with McNamara. Can be either a human or an automatic mechanical device, both of which, unlike the scarecrow, make noises. Simplest is a boy clapping two pieces of flat wood together.

boko – human head.

bone: 'I've got a bone in my leg' – an adult excuse offered to a child as a reason for not stirring from a chair.

bont – burnt; burned. **'As bad bont as scolt'** – as bad burned as scalded. Either of the available alternatives will bring pain or disadvantage. Used in situations of any magnitude, from job-changing and matrimonial prospects to deciding which domino to play next.

booby – childish or weak person. Also, the 'booby' or 'booby prize' is what is given to the competitor finishing a poor last.

books – (rhymes with spooks) magazines and periodicals, as distinct from newspapers. Actual books are called either school books or reading books.

boss – schoolmaster or employer. 'You can't do too much for a good boss' – an encouragement to workmates to keep up the pace. The customary rejoinder is, 'No, and you can't do too little for a bad bugger.'

bost, bosted – burst.

bost yer sen – burst yourself. Work until stopped by fatigue.

bote – bolt. The one on the door, and also what the horse does if the stable door's left open.

bottle – smell strongly and unpleasantly, especially as of something rotting. 'Them onions don't half bottle.' See hum.

bourn-shecker – bone-shaker. An old bicycle.

brambles – wild blackberries, either the bush or the fruit thereof. From the fruit are made bramble pies, bramble jam, bramble jelly and bramble crumbles, for which thanks be to God, and the devil take anybody as pulls down bramble hedges, thus reducing the sum of human happiness. Also, the playing-card suit commonly called clubs.

brand, spanking new – new, without doubt.

brangling – arguing.

brat – unwanted or troublesome child.

bread-and-cheese – the newly-opened leaves of hawthorn in spring; very tasty.

bread and pullit – plain bread, when there is nothing to adorn it. 'All the jam's done, and you had the cheese yisty; so it looks like it's bread and pullit while Friday.'

bread and same – dry bread, or bread with lard on in place of butter or margarine.

bread and scrat – bread with but a mere suggestion of margarine. 'She puts it on then scrats it off again.'

bread-slicer – helicopter.

breed – the width of work done at one pass by a tool or implement in linear motion. 'We s'll finish harvest a day sooner; this combine's got a two-foot wider breed than the old 'un.' Also, a good telling-off: 'If he does that once more, begoe I'm off to let him have a breed.'

breeks – breeches, which, with leather leggings and boots, were a popular covering for the lower parts of farm workers. Applied facetiously to ladies' knickers.

broad: 'It's as broad as it's long' – considering the argument in either of two ways, the outcome is similar.

broadcasting – sowing seed by scattering from the hand over an area of land, not in rows.

brock in – broken in. Made readily usable by an initial period of training or usage. Originally of horses, but extended to include boots, gardens, tractors, wives, apprentices, etc.

brock the back on it – broken the back of it. Of a task, the larger or most difficult part has been done.

broggling – poking; making, enlarging or clearing an orifice by pushing and/or rotating a stick or other object into it. 'This sink's blocked again, where's my broggler?'

brow – bough of a tree. Rhymes with cow.

brung – brought.

brusseling, sprouting – harvesting Brussels sprouts.

brussel-tops – the leafy crowns of the Brussels sprouts; discarded by the fastidious but cooked and eaten with relish by the thrifty.

brustles – bristles of a brush.

bubbed – of a bird's egg, containing a developed embryo, thus rendering it impossible to blow.

Buff's treat – annual children's party and outing organised by the local lodge of the Royal Antediluvian Order of Buffaloes—and they gave us all an orange and a bun.

bug – smug, pleased, self-satisfied with one's position or achievement. Sometimes 'rare and bug.'

bully – bullace, or sloe. We had a lane where they grew wild and we called it Bully Lane.

bumming – method of personal propulsion practised by some young children pending mastery of crawling or walking. 'He bummed all ower till he was eighteen months old.'

bung – cheese.

bun: got a bun in the oven – pregnant.

bunk-up – assistance from below whilst climbing.

burr round the moon – visible 'halo' due to atmospheric conditions. A sign of rain to come.

bus – any mechanically propelled vehicle. Frequently **'old bus'** – a sign of affection rather than an indication of age.

butt – a term used to cover any flat fish in the marshes.

butterslapper – grocer's assistant.

butting – gathering butts from the salt marsh.

butt-stanger – spiked weapon for catching butts.

C

cabbage stalks – derisive name applied to somebody who attempts to make an April fool of another outside the prescribed time, i.e. midnight to noon on the first of April.

cack-handed – left-handed, even if normally skilful; but also applied to somebody displaying clumsiness with either hand.

cady – innocently affectionate, usually said of a small child or animal.

cake – coward.

calling – uttering abuse or slander. People complaining of being called may be told: 'Sticks and stones may break your bones, but calling never hurts you.'

caning – causing to work hard, usually of apparatus or machinery. 'I could hear your tractor calling out; you wadn't half caning it.' A heavy smoker might be said to be 'Caning the owd Woodbines.'

can't wock: 'You can't wock a dead hoss' – the means of achieving the desired end are inadequate. The implement/machinery is worn out, or the procedure obsolete.

cap a donkey – something remarkable or unexpected is said to do this; so is a person whose behaviour is generally unusual or contrary.

capital – very good; excellent; eminently suitable; in the best of health.

caps owt – exceeds anything; an exclamation of astonishment.

cart: 'in the cart' – in trouble; encountering difficulties. 'It onny wants to come on to rain now and we s'll be well in the cart.'

cart-track – unmade road; sometimes a public way and sometimes farm or estate property. Often repaired with loose gravel or granite chips.

cat-ice – ice formed on a drain, but below which the water-level has fallen.

cat-in-hell: 'Not a cat-in-hell's chance' – in the speaker's opinion, the cause is without hope.

catching – infectious. Extended to things other than diseases: yawning, giggling, stammering, becoming pregnant, mispronouncing, tripping, committing minor errors, etc. are said to be catching.

causey – rhymes with horsey. Backyard of a house.

caution – person who may be expected to do slightly outrageous things. 'We'll have to ask Dan to come; he was a proper caution last time.'

cestun – cistern. The underground well in the yard into which rainwater from the house roof is directed. Even after the mains tap arrived in the yard, this water often continued to wash both clothes and people.

Water was drawn up with the cestun-bucket, having a rope tied to its handle. The square capping of ours, with a round hole in the middle to take the lid, was made of limestone; so the edges got worn where Dad sharpened kitchen knives.

champing – chewing, masticating. Old people often practise between meals.

chanch – chance.

chapel hat-pegs – human eyes, widely open thus giving the appearance of standing out: the result of amazement. Also, a measure of protrusion, as in one version of the poem about the blacksmith: 'And the muscles of his brawny arms stood out like chapel hat-pegs.'

chats – small potatoes, not for human consumption.

chatty – infested with fleas or bugs.

chauntering – muttering, grumbling. 'What's he chauntering about now?'

checkies – pigs.

cheern – chain. 'Mairk us a dairsy-cheern.'

cheers – chairs.

chelp – cheek; back-chat; out-of-turn or out-of-place talk. 'You'll be out of here quick, if you hev much more o' that chelp.'

cheps – the lower part of the face, especially with reference to the tatie-trap.

chesty – vulnerable to respiratory infections. 'Their youngest nivver wocked on the land because of being chesty.'

chewing the fat – arguing something out; discussing exhaustively.

no chicken – not young.

chimbly – chimney.

chippers – potatoes suitable for the fried chips trade.

chits – seed potatoes with shoots growing: the shoots.

chitter – chatter.

chitting-box – stackable slatted wooden tray for seed potatoes.

chittlings – chitterlings; pig's inner tubes, i.e. small intestines.

chock full; chock bang full – undoubtedly full.

'Chock up, chicken!' – choke up, chicken; said to someone, especially a child, who coughs or 'chokes' over food.

choice – choosy, fastidious, possessive. 'I wouldn't lend her owt as I was choice about.'

chop – switch the attention or opinion from one thing to another, especially if done frequently. 'You're always chopping and changing.'

chucked in – resigned; finished; left; opted out. 'He was treasurer of our pig club till he chucked in, last year.'

chuckies – hens.

chump – person who behaves foolishly or irresponsibly. Mild, and most often applied in cases of momentary lapses.

chunter; chaunter – grumble, especially in a quiet voice.

churchyarder – distressing cough.

clagging – clinging mud. 'Wipe them boots; we dooan't want that clagging all ower the house!'

claggy undernean – whatever the current weather, the ground is wet and muddy.

clamming – gathering clams (shellfish) from the salt marsh.

clamp – open-air potato store; a long heap of potatoes covered with straw and earth to protect from frost. (See grave).

clat – fuss, trouble. 'Don't clat about with tea for us; ours'll be waiting.'

clats – food requiring elaborate preparation. Also medications, especially homespun ones. 'She's nivver raight, allus tecking clats o' one sort or another.'

clawhammer coat – tailed coat worn by undertakers.

clawt – claw, as a cat does.

clean up – consume all food available at a meal. 'Can't anybody clean up that bit of pudding?'

clear as mud – comment on something not comprehended. A response to an attempted but unsuccessful explanation: 'Thank you; it's as clear as mud now.'

clees – claws; finger-nails.

clen; clent – cleaned.

cletch – clutch; originally of eggs but applied to most things. Often implies a larger quantity than expected. 'We didn't expect many folk, but quite a cletch turned up.'

clock – seed head of the dandelion, supposedly telling the time of day by the number of puffs needed to blow all the seeds off it. Also, to deliver a blow to the face as threatened in the phrase, 'I'll clock you one.'

clodhopper – facetious or faintly derogatory term for a farm worker. Anybody big, simple and clumsy.

closet – lavatory. Often at the opposite end of the garden from the house, and ivy-clad.

clover-knobs – dried clover flowers, said to make a good smoke in a clay pipe.

club – money received in compensation for loss of earnings due to sickness. Includes state benefit as well as that from contributory schemes, friendly societies, trade unions and local sick-and-dividing clubs. 'We can't afford it till we get the club.'

club: in the club; in the pudding-club – pregnant.

club book – mail order catalogue.

club day – local friendly societies' annual procession and field–day.

club night – name applied to Dad's night at the pub, so called because a club meeting was often cited as a reason for going. Any Dad who belonged to several (Oddfellows, Buffs, Foresters, sick-and-dividing, darts, pig, etc) could escape almost any evening. Mam's comment might be faintly cynical, 'Off out? Oh, aye – club night, I suppose!'

club together – raise a fund by mutual contribution for some specific benign or charitable purpose. 'There was no bus shelter down yon end of the village, so they clubbed together and had one put up.'

clunch – uncommunicative or secretive, but not necessarily sullen. 'He's a bit clunch, but not bad when you get to know him.'

clutter; clutterment – things left in disarray, especially if causing a nuisance.

cob – fruit-stone.

cobbles – coal in small lumps of roughly equal size.

cockly – unstable. Said of things not standing firmly or evenly on their bases, legs or wheels. Also, of a piece of furniture of which the structural soundness is suspect.

coco mat – matting made of coconut fibres. The fibres being smooth, dirt and dust passed through and it needed but a brief shake to clean it. Then spread old newspapers on the floor to catch the next lot. Popular in tiled-floor kitchens used as main thoroughfares between hearth and garden.

code – cold.

cod frozz – cold frozen; very cold of a person. 'Come on in agen the fire; you look cod frozz.'

collared rind – brawn.

collared-rind pits – legendary mine-workings at Kirton End, from which collared-rind (brawn) was supposedly extracted. This is a local joke akin to the Cheshire Treacle-mines, or Ken Dodd's Jam-butty mines at Knotty Ash. I heard 'Kirton End collared-rind pits' mentioned as far afield as Folkingham, in the 1930s.

colus – coalhouse.

come into – inherited: goods as well as money. Applied also to less conventional modes of acquisition e.g., having fallen off a lorry.

come over – happened to. 'She's nivver done owt like it afore; what's come over her?' (See also gotten into.)

come-day, go-day – lackadaisical.

company – social visitor(s) to the house. Offspring visiting whilst resident elsewhere are not company, neither are lodgers or other habitual dwellers. But parents are when they make rare, invited visits to offspring, and so are uncles, aunts, nieces, nephews, cousins, grandparents and friends. When there is company in, a neighbour used to popping in frequently will decline to do so: 'I'm sorry, I didn't know you had company.' (See front door company)

confab – conference of two or more people.

conk – human nose, especially a large one.

conk; conk' out – cease to function for mechanical reasons. 'I'd have been done well afore dark, onny the tractor kep conking out.'

conker – horse chestnut, both the noble tree and the nut itself. The conker season begins in September with collecting, proceeds to boring and stringing, then climaxes in the actual game called conkers. The author's best performance was a 'niner', ie a conker which broke nine adversaries before meeting its match.

conqueror – deciding game betwen competing players, after preceding play has resulted in equality.

contrary – rhymes with Mary and describes behaviour or argument which is wifully obstructive or unorthodox. Also applied to a person habitually behaving thus: 'He's such a contrary devil to deal with.'

cop: not much cop – of little use or value.

cop hold of – take into the hand or hands.

copper – round, open-topped metal vessel with wooden lid, ten gallons capacity, set in brickwork three feet square in a corner of the wash-house. A coal fire lit below at 5.30 a.m. on Monday had the first of the wash boiling by 7.00 a.m. if the wind was right. A similar model outdoors was for boiling pig-tates. Also called a cauden.

coppernob – person with ginger hair.

copper shovel – short, narrow -bladed coal shovel for the copper fire.

'Couldn't hit a barn wall if he stood inside it' – said of a poor marksman.

cow: 'Like the cow's tail' – said of one who is perpetually unable to maintain an expected rate of work and is 'always behind.'

cowardy custard – a display of timidity calls forth the jingle: 'Cowardy, cowardy custard; eat more mustard!'

crack up – speak well of. 'He cracks his sen up' means that he blows his own trumpet. Anything falling short of reputed quality is 'Not what it's cracked up to be.' Also, to be overcome by spontaneous laughter: 'When she said that, it med me crack up.'

cram-jam – full to capacity.

craunch – harsh grating sound as of heavy object in sliding contact with another. 'I see Bill's car's had a row with his gatepost; bet that was a craunch.' Also, the sound of apples or potato crisps eaten.

craw – crow or rook.

crawler – track-laying tractor. Also called a Caterpillar, which is a brand name.

creaking gate – person who is often ill, or has a chronic malaise or disability. Observing that such people sometimes outlive the apparently healthy: 'It's the crearking gairt as swings the longest.'

create – make a fuss. 'What a mess! Mam'll create when she sees it.'

creesort – creosote.

crew – body of people of whom the speaker disapproves, especially in the political sense. 'The M.P. was there, and all the usual crew.'

crocked up – disabled by injury or illness.

crookled – crooked; things, but not people.

cross as two sticks – out of temper, peevish.

crossbar – ride as a passenger on a bicycle, side-saddle on the horizontal frame-tube. 'Are you off my road? Give us a crossbar!'

crosses! – to cry this during a game means 'I have my fingers crossed.' A truce is in force, which the other players are expected to honour.

cross-oppled – confused, especially in argument. Led astray by the introduction of spurious factors. Or a person may 'Get theirsens cross-oppled' if experiencing difficulty with a solo task.

crosspatch – peevish or short-tempered person.

crow – boast; talk over-confidently.

crutches – spectacles.

cry : 'Don't cry afore you're hurt' – don't be too hasty with objections.

cuddy – hedge-sparrow; dunnock.

cuffing – smoking cigarettes, as distinct from 'puffing' a pipe. 'I see you're still cuffing away at the owd Woodbines.'

cullinder – colander.

cultivators – steam-driven ploughing engines, using winches and cables to draw a plough back and forth across a field.

Cunningsby – the 'proper' spelling is Coningsby (my misspelling is to indicate pronunciation). Other place-names sound thus: Aljercock (Algarkirk); Suddy-un (Sutterton); Olbij (Holbeach); Iddick (Eaudyke); Dunny-un (Donington); Frisskunny (Friskney); Owd Lee-ack (Old Leake); Bullinbruck (Bolingbroke); Billinger (Billinghay); and everybody's favourite place Skegsnest.

D

dab-and-sucker – from all good goody-shops, one penny (pre-1939). A triangular paper bag containing kali; protruding from one corner a blackjack (liquorice) tube. You could bite off the sealed end of the tube and suck up the kali powder at the risk of making yourself cough, or prolong the delight by dabbing and sucking.

dab hand – one skilled at a particular task or game. 'She's a dab hand on the bowling green.' Also called a dabster.

dacker; dacker down – reduce speed, or become less active. Of moving but inanimate things, allowed to slow by inertia. 'He didn't brake, he just took his foot off and was dackering down.' 'He still wocks, although the doctor warned him to dacker down a bit.'

daft: too daft to laugh at – criticism of comedy which oversteps credibility.

daft as a handcart – silly. The very silly are daft as a brush; extreme cases daft as a boiled owl.

dainty – fussy or choosy over food, especially if the intake is thought to be insufficient. 'You can't just put owt in front of her like you can Bill. She's a bit dainty.'

daisy-pushing – dead and buried.

dake – dyke.

David: 'Send it down, David (or Moses)' – encouragement uttered for no apparent reason during heavy rain or snowfall.

dawn – down, from birds. Any light, soft loose material is said to be dawny.

dead beat; deat bet – tired, exhausted.

dead agen – dead against; strongly opposed to. 'All on us round here is dead agen having a Marketing Board'.

dead duck – something previously of significance which no longer need be considered. 'The old Parish Meeting's a dead duck now.'

deal – comparative measure, generally used to denote lesser magnitude.

'Not a great deal.' 'She doesn't ail a deal' (is healthy).

Derbac – proprietary brand of soap for the hair, used to discourage vermin.

dick-comb – fine-toothed comb to remove vermin from the head.

diddlum – kind of lottery.

difference: 'If there's any difference they're both alike' – they are identical.

dig your heels in – maintain your position or opinion in argument.

dilly-cart – horse-drawn vehicle employed by the Council to collect night soil – the contents of bucket lavatories. An intermediate stage between do-it-yourself burial and the arrival of mains sewerage in the nineteen-fifties.

ding in – teach with difficulty.

dingy – (rhymes with stingy) dull or drab in appearance.

dinner – meal taken at or near to midday, whatever it consists of.

dinner-bag – Some children walked several miles to school when bicycles were a luxury. School meals in those days were not a luxury, they were science-fiction, so enough food had to be brought to keep the engine going through a long day. It was brought in a dinner-bag. Not a satchel; those were for High and Grammar School pupils who homeworked and carried books. Dad's dinner-bag was a khaki ex-army sidepack, the school one a scaled-down version of it.

dinnertime – the middle of the day; any time around 12.00 noon.

dint – dent

dither – shiver with cold. Also, 'to dither about' is to be undecided.

dob – small quantity of something liquid or pasty. Application of paint with a brush, poking rather than stroking.

dock; dockin – weed with large leaves and a long white root like a parsnip. There are legends about root depth, some involving Australia. Rubbing the crushed leaf on a nettle-sting brings relief. Notoriously difficult to eradicate from a garden: 'Even if you bonn it, the smoork teks root.'

doctored – rendered unable to reproduce, by means of surgery.

'It doesn't like me' – said of food which the speaker would enjoy, but which is known to cause discomfort.

dog: 'If you keep a dog, you don't do your own barking' – having hired somebody for a particular task, you don't do it yourself.

dog-daisies – stinking mayweed.

don't: 'They don't shame their keep' – said of a family who look well nurtured, often as a compliment to the president of the kitchen.

'It's not fit to turn a dog out' – the weather is vile.

dogs – sausages.

dog's dinner – standard of sartorial excellence. 'Where's he off to, all done up like a dog's dinner?'

dole money – money received or expected from local charities. In our village it was distributed in the Parish Hall on Dole Day, in mid-December.

dollop – a lump of anything of soft consistency.

dolly – wooden implement for agitating the clothes in the dolly-tub. It was shaped like a four-legged stool but with a pole rising vertically from its centre, and a cross-handle. Superseded by the posher which was more scientific, whatever that means.

dolsh – large quantity or helping. 'Let's have a good dolsh o' that pudding.'

done a bit at – damaged. 'That storm did a bit at the corn.'

done: 'That's done him one' – that has scored a point over him.

done in – killed, either by accident or design. A suicide is said to have 'Done his (her) sen in.'

doo – no! Most emphatically not.

doodah – gadget or contrivance unnamed, or of which the name is forgotten. A variation is dooflip, or a how's-your-father.

doorstep; doorstop – thick slice of bread with, for the lucky, a proportionate thickness of margarine or dripping. The rich got butter, the stupendously rich butter *and* jam.

dost; dossunt – dare; dare not. 'I dost climb up there any time.' 'I bet you dossunt tell him so.'

dot-and-carry-one – lame person.

doted; doty – going bad, especially of fruit. Apples stored under the bed in winter occasionally doted if they were put away bruised, and had to be picked out with the aid of a keen nose and a candle.

dots – dominoes.

double shuffle – anybody working or moving faster than their custom is 'doing a double shuffle.'

dow – rhymes with cow and means no, emphatically or scornfully.

down below – in the Wash in a small boat.

drat – a mild expletive, permissible in most vicarages.

draw – of tea; brew or mash. The process of turning boiling water into tea includes a pleasantly anticipatory period of waiting for the magical transformation: this is known as 'letting it draw.'

drawing out nicely – what nights are said to be doing in late winter and early spring, meaning that darkness falls later. The autumnal comment, 'Nights draws in' is laden with foreboding.

dreckly– directly; almost immediately; as soon as possible. 'I've nearly done making the beds; I'll be down dreckly.'

dressmaker: 'Like a dressmaker' – measure of the urgency with which personal relief is required. 'I want to pee like a dressmaker.'

drifting – shooing away unwanted cats, dogs, or children from the vicinity of the house. 'That's the third time today I've drifted that dog off our garden.'

drink – liquid prepared for drinking, as contrasted with plain water. 'I don't want water, I want drink.' In summer there was lemonade made from crystals weighed out into white paper bags at the sweet-shop; herb beer; tea hot or cold; coffee from a bottle; or, to protect against exposure, an egg bet (beaten) up in hot milk. 'Drink' is also a faintly condemnatory reference to alcohol.

dripping-tin – shallow metal vessel to hold meat in the oven.

driv – driven; drove. 'I driv cultivators thotty-fower year.'

drop a line – write a letter.

drove – a lot of people. 'About every other Sunday we got a whole drove o' relations tonning up for dinner.'

drover – man who drove sheep and cattle on foot from farm to market. The title is not inherited by drivers of lorries.

drunk as a fiddler's bitch – exceptionally drunk.

duck-fit – outburst of exasperation or anger. 'If the gaffer sees that gairt left open he'll hev a duck-fit.'

duckfoot – type of horse-drawn hoe. Also, one of its tines.

duck-frost – rain. Especially a wry reference to a day on which frost had been promised or expected but which turned out wet.

ducks and drakes – the game of throwing suitable stones to skim across the surface of water.

duck's disease – 'ailment' said to be suffered by one lacking in stature, the clearance between ground and posterior being dangerously small.

dundy – dull, colourless, unexciting.

dunty – excrement.

dust: 'You won't see him for dust!' – he will depart rapidly.

dust you wait – just you wait, threateningly.

Dutch – incomprehensible. 'I see the notice on the board, but it was all Dutch to me.' Double Dutch is even worse.

Dutch: 'The Dutch has took Holland' – whimsical response to 'What's the news?'

dyke-sider – advanced form of courtship practised on the sloping side of a dyke.

dyking; daking – clearing or digging out dykes.

duck: 'Like a dying duck in a thunderstorm' – said of someone showing little interest or animation.

E

ears burning – 'If your ears burn, somebody's talking about you.' The word 'burning' is used figuratively.

eau – almost a disused word except when included in a geographical name. Rivers are rivers, drains drains, dykes dykes and small channels grips. Ditch is rare; lode, leam and delph exotic.

eckups – hiccups.

ended – broken; spoilt; wrecked; written off. 'Dooan't say that gel's gone and ended another bike!'

enew – enough. 'I'd say it's all of two mile: I ought to know, I've walked it times enew.'

engine-driver: 'When I speak to the engine-driver, I don't expect an answer from his oily rag' – remark of the same order as the organ-grinder and his monkey; a whimsical (though perhaps seriously intended) request that the party addressed should reply, not someone electing to do so on their behalf.

'elevenpence-ha'penny short of a bob' – lacking mental capacity.

eppen – adroit; skilled. Not much used; but a lot of people get themselves described as 'strange and uneppen.'

eppon – apron; anything worn as such. A hessian bag becomes an eppon if tied round the waist in a wet vegetable field.

esquire – a title sometimes bestowed in belittling fashion. A rhyme may be added: 'John Smith, Esquire, dead 'oss and donkey buyer.'

ewse – use.

eyes – spectacles.

F

fairish – considerable, especially meaning big or heavy. 'He's got a fairish owd jag on thon waggon.'

fairther; fayther – father. Even used as the second word of the Lord's prayer.

fasswelted – condition of a sheep which has accidentally rolled on to its back and is unable to rise.

fate – fight.

feed – quantity of vegetables, usually meaning the amount eaten by a family at one meal. During harvest, workers might be permitted to 'take a feed'; indeed, some assert the practice to be established by custom.

fierce; fierce as a lop – vivacious; lively. 'What is it you feed your lot on? They're allus fierce.'

find a good home for – eat. 'Can't anybody find a good home for that last sausage?'

fire 'Somebody had a fire?' – a person in new clothes or on a new bicycle might be thus chaffingly greeted. The reference is to the cheap selling-off of goods after a shop or warehouse fire; the implication, that the buyer is perhaps a shade too mean to pay full price.

fish: 'He's a big fish in a little pond' – he might be of consequence in parish pump affairs, but put him in a town or city . . .

fit to knock a man off a horse – smelling strongly.

five-and-twenty – twenty-five, when telling the time.

five-bar – field gate constructed with five horizontals.

fizzog – face, especially one less than handsome.

flaring about – gadding; pursuing pleasure; attending numerous social functions. 'She was still flaring about, years after she got married.'

flees – flies.

flies – what astute or knowledgeable people are said not to have on them.

flit – move house. A moonlight flit is an overnight move to a secret destination, usually to avoid paying debts or facing scandal.

flock – bits of wool and shredded cloth used to stuff a mattress.

flummoxed – perplexed; bewildered. 'I've read the instructions fower times and I'm still flummoxed.'

fly – astute; cunning; not to be trusted. 'He's a fly devil; I wouldn't let him hev hode o' none o' my money.'

fog – first. Called as a claim to be first to play in a game eg. marbles. 'Two's up, fog!' (See seg, lag, and tuzzy-muzzy).

foggy underfoot – comment on the wetness of the ground.

folks – parents.

fool: 'He's a fool to his sen' – his behaviour is against his own ultimate benefit.

no forrader – no further forward; no progress has been made. 'We talked all morning and ended up no forrader.'

forruds – forwards.

fost – first. Fost off is early in the morning. 'It was a bit owery fost off.'

fotnit – fortnight.

four cross roads – place where two roads cross. If a road joins another without crossing, it is a three cross roads.

four-eyes – person wearing glasses.

fower – four; rhymes with mower.

frit – frightened.

frizzy – description of human hair which stands out from the head.

frocklifter – male with an inclination for disturbing female apparel. More seriously, a philanderer.

frog-march – enforced propulsion of man by man by holding his wrist and ankle on one side and causing him to hop along.

front door company; front room company – Visitors whose social standing demands that they be admitted at the front door and entertained in the front room. Family, friends, close neighbours, tradesmen and most relatives use the back door: vicars, schoolmasters, squires and doctors would expect the front one to be opened. Employers, of whatever magnitude, generally go to the back.

froz; frez – frozen.

fruzzy – frizzy.

f.t.b.– fit to bust. More than satisfied after a good meal.

fuffoo-valve – any mysterious or uncomprehended piece of technical apparatus. A motorist with his head in his (car) bonnet might be asked, 'Is it the fuffoo-valve gone again?'

full of emptiness – definitely empty.

full of him (her) self – said of people who are their own favourite topic.

fumigating – burning scraps of paper in a sick-room to kill foul smells.

fun – found. 'Cheer up. You look as if you lost a bob and fun sixpence.'

furbill – hedge-knife.

G

gaffer – on a big farm, the foreman. The owner would be known as the guv'nor or Mr Jones; his son as Mr Dick. On a small farm the owner himself might be called the gaffer. 'Sir' is an alien word. To call an important gentleman gaffer is faintly disrespectful; it is done frequently.

gaffman – garthman; yard foreman.

gain – in close proximity. 'Don't plant too gain o' the hedge.'

gain a day, gain a friend – optimistic saying when in confusion over which day of the week it is.

gammy – of a leg, foot, arm or hand, crippled; either temporarily or permanently. 'Let Bill go up fost, with his gammy leg.'

gandling – talking in a rambling way; going on a bit.

gang – group of agricultural hand-workers, controlled by an entrepreneur called the ganger or gangmaster, who contracts with farmers for specific schedules of work to be done. The ganger's principal capital is the vehicle or vehicles in which the gangs are transported.

ganzy – short coat.

gapping – removing unwanted plants from a row, using a hoe. (See singling.)

gawp – gaze; look intently, especially when regarded as impudent or intrusive. 'Do you have to stand gawping at me?'

gedge – bicycle, especially one old or decrepit. Rarely applied to any other wheeled vehicle.

gelling – girling; a teenage occupation for males; walking streets or visiting likely places, viewing the opposite sex with critical hopefulness. Strictly for the unattached. 'He don't gò gelling now; he's courting.'

gen – (g as in gun) gave. 'I gen him a few tairts.' Also, given: 'Has she gen you any tea?'

geower – give over! desist! Also, given over: a query about whether the rain has stopped might sound like 'Ezzit geower?'

gev – gave.

giddy-goat – a flighty person; one of unpredictable behaviour.

giddy half-hour – period of effervescent, high-spirited play, useful at a child's bedtime in burning up the residue of the day's energy.

give over – stop working; not necessarily having finished but because time or economic considerations have intervened.

gleany – descriptive of pale sunlight in humid air. Thought to herald rain or thunder.

gleg – look; take a quick glance; examine. 'Let's have a gleg at your bad knee.'

glory-hole – storage space for things that might come in handy sometime; dark cupboard; the space behind the garden shed. Washing-machines and central heating have converted many washhouses and coal-houses into glory-holes.

go – travel fast. 'We didn't half go, coming this way.'

goat – the abstract thing which is 'got' when the temper is lost or the patience tried. 'It gets my goat, hearing folk talk like that.'

gob-stopper – big, hard goodie (boiled sweet).

godger – gooseberry.

gog – spit; spittle.

gogs – goggles; spectacles.

going at it; going at it a good 'un – working hard and purposefully; walking quickly; playing a game well.

in going gear – active; fit for action. 'Our gran's tonned eighty, and still in going gear.'

gollop – eat or drink quickly and noisily. 'Doan't gollop your dinner down like that there.'

go mad – overspend. 'I went mad today and bought a new hat.'

gone on – keen about; in favour of. Usually negative: 'I'm not all that gone on the pictures; I'd as soon stop at hom with the wireless.'

goo; gooer – go. A popular snatch of dialogue pokes gentle fun at the pronunciation; it is from a supposed game of 'domino out', played in pubs, with somebody called Joe. The game is won when a player puts down his last piece and calls 'domino'. 'Can yer gooer, Jooer?' 'Nooer.' Click. 'Dominooer!'

a good cup – strong tea.

goodies – sweets, as bought from a confectioner.

good rough owd – phrase signifying robust worth. A good rough owd bike is one which can be ridden anywhere and relied upon.

good shuts – good riddance.

goofy – unconsciously silly.

goosegogs – gooseberries.

got done at – sacked from; ceased employment at. 'He's never worked since he got done at Manor Farm.'

got off with – clicked; struck up an instant (amorous) relationship with.

gotten – got; obtained; in possession of. 'Reckon I've gotten a touch of the owd screws.'

gotten Into – entered. 'What's gotten into him?' means why is he behaving thus?

got up: 'I got up before I went anywhere' – I rose exceptionally early.

gowt – outfall or junction of waterway (rare except in place-names).

goy! – exclamation of surprise or emphasis.

granny's bonnet – Aquilegia, a garden flower.

Grandma Navenby – Sets of grandparents are distinguished from each other by adding their place of residence instead of the surname.

grave – heap of vegetables stored outdoors, suitably protected. Main-crop potato graves were run alongside lanes, to facilitate winter loading. Also called clamps.

Great: The Great I Am – nickname for a self-opinionated person.

green: 'He's not so green as he's cabbage-looking' – he is more astute than might be supposed.

gress – grass. And a gress widder is a lady temporarily deprived of her husband's company.

gret – great. Used to emphasise either magnitude or quality: a 'gret garden' might be either a large or a well-tended one.

grewill – gruel.

grid – bicycle.

grip – narrow, open drainage channel cut with a spade.

grizzle – grumble or complain in a low-powered, monotonous manner. A child's incoherent discontented half-crying is called grizzling.

grouse – grumble, complain; also, the subject of complaint. 'Anybody's got a grouse, they come and see me.'

grubbing about – searching or working in a dirty or dark place.

gruft – dirt ingrained into the skin. 'I've gev my hands a good wesh, but they still look grufty.'

grun – ground, as in a corn mill.

grunssle – groundsel.

grussle – gristle, as in meat.

'Gulls are in!' – large numbers of seagulls have flown inland, said to be a sign of bad weather to come. They are unreliable.

gun – person with a gun, attending an organised shoot. 'It was a poor field today; onny eight guns tonned up.'

guzzle – drink eagerly.

Gyrotiller – large machine for deep cultivation

H

hacing – raining very slightly. 'It's not really raining just hacing about.'

hackle – cough. 'That's a nasty hackle; let me get you a dose of jollop.'

hackles – 'Don't get your hackles up' means don't let your temper flare.

had: been had – been tricked or swindled.

had up – summoned to appear in a court.

haft – handle of tool or implement.

hairiff – goosegrass, growing wild in hedgerows. The seeds cling to fur and clothing, and are called sweethearts.

half-a-past – half past the hour.

half-masters – trousers with unusually short legs, often eliciting the greeting, 'Hello, who's passed away, then?'

half sharp – not very bright mentally. Usually 'Not quite half sharp' or 'Not above half sharp.'

hammel – hovel; small lean-to on the side of a larger building.

hanging: 'See owt hanging, pull it!' – playful reference, sometimes accompanied by appropriate action, to another's loose clothing or stray lock of hair. With less delicacy, given jocularly to a lady as advice to be followed on her wedding-night.

hankacher – handkerchief.

harden – hessian; sackcloth; coarse fabric. Used as backing for snip-rugs.

harder: 'It's harder where there's none' – Mam's response to a complaint about bread crust being hard.

hap – wrap or cover, especially as protection against cold.

harrud; harrowed – very tired physically. 'Let's stop a bit and get set down; I'm about harrowed.'

harm – haulm; the visible part of a growing root-crop, especially potatoes.

hawking – clearing the throat noisily.

headlands – strips of an arable field at the ends of crop rows, in which horses or tractors are turned.

headwork – work requiring thought or scholarship; office work. 'I s'll learve it to you to wock out; I've never been one for no headwork.'

heard tell – heard; was told; overheard. The telling of a piece of juicy gossip, perhaps slightly embroidered, ends with 'So I've heard tell.'

heared – heard. 'I've never heared nowt like it!'

hearth-rug – the one occupied by (left to right) Mam's feet, the cat, Dad's feet. Invariably a snip-rug manufactured on site from old clothing cut into snip-length strips, sorted into colours according to pattern, and pulled through the harden with a pegger.

Heaven help the sailor (on a night like this)' – comment on inclement weather, particularly a gale.

heavy – hot, of an object picked up carelessly whilst hot, then hastily dropped again. It was said of a blacksmith's apprentice, 'The fost thing he learns is what's heavy.'

hedging and ditching – the twin staple tasks of the farm worker in slack or growing seasons, cutting down unwanted growth. Now largely done by powered attachments on tractors. *Punch* once had a cartoon depicting a huge contraption labelled 'The Acme Hedger and Ditcher; Does the Work of Three Men and a Boy.' Operating it were a boy and three men.

Heinz – dog of indeterminate breed; after a food manufacturer whose advertising slogan was '57 Varieties'.

heet! – instruction to a horse to turn leftward.

Hell Fen End –wry name for a place looking bleak and cheerless.

helped up – handicapped by an overload of current obligations. 'I can't do it, not while I'm helped up with all these kids.'

herb – man, especially one of unusual character or behaviour. 'He's a rum herb, that one.'

hern – hers.

hesh – give a good hiding. 'I'll hesh you at playtime.'

hicking stick – stout stick of ash, two feet long, used by two men behind a sackful of potatoes, to enable it to be swung upward on to a wagon or lorry. Also called a jack.

hiller – tatie ridger; tool for raising soil from between crop rows to form a ridge for the plants to grow out of.

hill-sitting (or ill-sitting) hen – Of a person who habitually moves from place to place, either indoors on a particular day or between localities during life, it is said: 'He's like a hill-sitting hen; he's easy nowhere.'

hill up – draw soil from between crop rows to around the growing plants.

his'n – his.

hit on – discover; invent; encounter by chance.

hobbing iron – cast iron last for supporting footwear during repair. Also called a snobbing iron.

hod – heard. 'Have you hod the lairtest?'

hode – hold.

hoddle; oddle – finger stall; covering to protect a wounded finger. Discarded gloves and broken bootlaces were kept to provide materials for the making of hoddles.

holden – beholden; obliged to. 'He telled me, but I took no notice. I'm not holden to him.'

hold your hosses; hold hard – cease; desist; stop. Used in both physical and abstract senses; eg to halt a speaker in debate because he is overlooking something important.

hom; ooerm – home.

hom-it! oerm-it – home it! Go home! Gruff, threatening dismissal of an intruding cat or dog; occasionally of a child.

hoody – pronounced huddy; the game of hide-and-seek. To get hoody is to hide.

hook: 'take your hook' – 'go'.

hooker – large specimen.

hoop (and skimmer) – Each cost a shilling, which included the entertainment of watching the blacksmith make them. The hoop was an iron rod bent to a circle the size of a bike wheel, and joined; the skimmer a hook to propel, steer and stop the rolling hoop. An expert could travel for miles trotting nonchalantly beside his hoop and touching it deftly now and then to hold speed and course. My only hoop went out of control, swerved into a drain and was lost for ever.

hoping – 'hoping this finds you'. Letters to family invariably began 'Hoping this finds you well, as it leaves us at present . . .' followed, if there was any doubt, by the qualification 'except that' (for relatively serious cases) or 'although' (for coughs, colds and bandaged fingers). The ending was signalled by 'I must close now, as . . .' followed by some pressing reason of a domestic nature which often took another two pages to describe. Finally, 'Your ever-loving . . . ' There are, apart perhaps from 'Cheers, then', no equivalents in telephone conversations.

hossacking – see ossacking.

hot – hurt. 'Hard work nivver hot nobody!'

hound – usually 'young hound'; mischievous or precocious child, though occasionally addressed to an adult wrongdoer.

home: 'He'll eat us out of house and home' – Jocular comment on an appetite which is healthy.

how's-your-father – used in the same way as 'doings' or 'doodah'; something the speaker can't remember the name of.

hum – smell strongly and unpleasantly.

humming and harring (rhymes with sparring) – talking indecisively; avoiding utterance of what ought to be said; talking instead of doing. 'Ain't no ewse standing there humming and harring; the job's got to be done.'

hump – carry.

hunch; haunch – cold. 'It's a bit hunch these mornings.'

hunking – big.

I

iddunt – isn't.

idle-backs – unwanted splinters of hard skin growing from beside the finger-nails; said to be due to an unfamiliarity with work.

'If the Lord spares us' – an habitual codicil to a statement of intention; a more profound version of 'all being well', or 'with a bit of luck'. 'We s'll be at market a Wednesday, if the Lord spares us.'

a good innings – a long life. Of somebody recently dead or expected to die: 'Ah, well, I suppose he's had a good innings.'

intek – intake. The flat table of land between the main channel of a stream or creek and the higher land level on either side. Some small houses used to stand on the inteks of our drain. People have cultivated inteks in the past without the formality of paying rent.

Irish – not making sense.

it – the player in the game of tag, locally called 'its', who must touch another player in order to pass on the status of being it.

J

jack – see hicking stick.

jack-hoe – manual implement, used mainly on gardens and allotments. It is pulled walking backwards, and the tines jack themselves into the soil to lift and crumble it.

jack in – leave a job or appointed office; cease to give help or support with a shared task.

jag – load, especially a heavy load on a vehicle. 'Yon lorry ain't half got a jag on.'

Jarge – George. Many names get variant pronunciations: Watson rhymes with Patson; Jessop with fizz-up.

jeese – rhymes with geese. Yes, emphatically.

jet – ladle; cylindrical metal vessel about half the size of a bucket and fitted with a long, oblique wooden handle. Used for removing the contents of vault lavatories, which had to be buried.

jiffle – fidget; make movements, especially when seated, to the annoyance of others. Persistence in doing so might earn the title 'jiffle-arse'.

jitty; jetty – path or short spur of unmetalled road giving access to one or more houses.

joggling-pin – almost any pin-like mechanical fastening or retaining device; linchpin on a waggon, cotter-pin on a bicycle, etc.

jollop – liquid medicine, mostly that designed to alleviate coughs.

jorped – warped or twisted.

jumble – unwanted domestic goods given for a charity jumble sale.

jumpdake; jumpdyke – a sheep. Also used facetiously for the meat thereof. 'Now then, can I cut anybody a slice more jumpdake?'

K

kapurtle – used by males to denote females in any quantity from one upwards, particularly those considered desirable or accessible or both. 'She's what I call a nice bit o' kapurtle.'

keb – sob.

keeps! – called before starting a game of marbles, to signify an agreement that winners keep winnings.

keep your hair on (wigs is dear) – don't lose your temper.

keck; kecksy – the tall, white-flowered summer roadside weed, called by some experts 'cow-parsley', to which other experts respond 'Rubbish!'. Other experts, pistols drawn, declare it to be hemlock. Or chervil. A keck-whistle is a musical instrument made from a dry, hollow keck-stalk with finger-holes cut in it.

kelch; keltch – descriptive of an object or substance which is intrinsically worthless. 'They're all plastic nowadays; load of Hong Kong kelch.'

kelly – marbles game played where playgrounds were too hard to make marble-holes. The kelly, a small skittle-shaped object, was shied at by the players, its proprietor keeping the misses and paying out an agreed quantity for the hits.

kelly lamp – small round domestic paraffin lamp in which the wick-fed flame is surrounded by a squat globular glass chimney. The base is weighted to return it upright if knocked over.

kelter – things left in disarray. Not necessarily rubbish, though there might be some included: toys, tools, the debris from some activity, are kelter. 'I hope you're going to clear up all this kelter before you go to bed.'

kep – kept. 'We allus kep a few fowls at one time.'

kifer – females, considered by males with a view to sexual adventure. Crumpet.

killer – slaughterer, especially of pigs. A freelance anybody could hire for the dirty deed, for which he attended the hirer's premises. Not always a butcher by trade; the know-how was handed down from father to son.

kindling – small pieces of wood or twigs suitable for igniting coal fires. Also, scrap wood which could be split into kindling.

knocked into the middle of next week – suggested fate awaiting a person under threat of violence. Also, a description of what has happened to an opportunity lost through misfortune.

knowed – known; knew.

L

labourer – agricultural worker not specialising in a particular job such as stockman or horseman. A misleading title: on a mixed farm raising not only stock but perhaps fifteen or twenty different crops within a few years, his knowledge was often considerably more extensive and complex than that of a factory labourer.

ladder: 'The fost time I went up a ladder was down a well' – an often quoted anonymous remark of an 'Irish' nature, which after thought is seen to be quite logical.

la-di-da – posh; affecting to be wealthy or superior.

Lady day – moving or flitting day: that appointed for farm workers to change their place of employment and/or residence. 25 March or (on some farms) 6 April.

lag – last, the final participant in a game in which players go in turn. See also fog, seg and tuzzy-muzzy.

laid up – ill; incapacitated. Used even when the patient is not in bed.

lairy – daft; light-headed.

lam; lam into – hit during a fist fight.

lambing shower – brief rainfall typical of spring.

lap – wrap; hap.

larn – learn, meaning teach. Used mostly when the lesson is to be on a particular aspect of behaviour. 'If I get hode o' that young hound I'll larn him to keep his tongue still.'

larraping – hitting with a whip or stick; usually a horse, but sometimes a child.

lay – wager; bet. 'I'll lay it'll rain afore we reach home.'

laying; layering – a particular way of trimming a thorn hedge, 'laying in' half-cut pieces to fill gaps. According to those versed in the craft, nobody ever does it properly any more.

lazy wind – a very cold one, usually north-easterly or easterly. 'It's a lazy wind; it dooan't stop to go round you, it goes straight through.'

leading – transporting produce from harvest field to rail depots, or into storage.

leanings – places to lean on, e.g. fences and bridges, to watch the world go by and gossip. In our village the hardest worked leaning was the churchyard wall, known at one end as the House of Commons.

leave it be; let it be – leave it alone; don't do any more to it. Also of a person who would be better not troubled or annoyed: 'She's teasing our Albert again; tell her to leave him be.'

let drive – talk forcefully, as when laying down the law. 'The gaffer come down the yard and see it, and by goy didn't he let drive!'

lether – ladder.

lickety-spit – descriptive of speed, of something travelling very quickly.

lig – liar.

light on – discover; find; encounter by chance. 'We went to the show, and who should we light on but owd Taylor from down the fen.'

lip: 'Don't trip ower your bottom lip!' – Don't wear such a woeful expression.

lit on – found.

little-'un – child of a family; the youngest if there are several. Also, offspring of farm or domestic animal.

living in – of an employee, most often a domestic servant, resident within the employer's house. Some farm workers lived in, as did apprentices to joiners, wheelwrights, blacksmiths and builders.

loadened – loaded; the act of loading completed.

lob – lean, or tilt. 'It dooan't stand up straight, it lobs ower like Surfleet tower.'

lont – learnt, meaning taught. 'I lont that owd devil a lesson he weearn't forget'.

look-up! – look out! Beware of danger; make way.

Lord Muck; Lady Muck (from Tod Hall) – titles bestowed, generally not within their hearing, on people apparently aspiring to a station above their own.

lotment – allotment; plot of land rented (usually from the local authority) for spare-time cultivation.

lotting – allotting; the farm foreman's daily task of deciding which men do which jobs.

low road – the way to somewhere, avoiding the main road. 'Let's tek our bikes and go low road.'

lug – carry, especially a basket or bag.

lumbered up – of a room or yard, left untidy. 'You can hardly tonn round in the plairce, lumbered up like that there.'

lump – tolerate.

lump of wood – measure of comparative speed, used of performance at work. 'Ain't you done that weeding yet? You're as slow as a lump of wood.'

lunch – mid-morning snack now called elevenses. The main midday meal, whatever its form, is dinner on both Sundays and weekdays. The afternoon or evening meal, even if a three-courser, is tea.

lurrum – pronounced lur-rum. Alarm clock. 'I was a bit late this morning; never hod the lurrum.'

M

mad – angry, annoyed.

made of money – rich. Usually negatively: 'We can't afford that; we ain't made of money.'

make-haste: on the make-haste – of a dealer or tradesman, overcharging; profiteering; trying to get rich quickly. Some did. Some still do.

make work with – damage. 'This rain'll make work with the corn.'

mam – mother. Everybody's mother is Mam; Mum is faintly upperclass, and Mummy infantile.

Mam's – my mother's house; the family homestead. So called by an offspring who has left it and gone to live elsewhere.

Mam: 'Your Mam wants your boots to put your Dad's beer in' – a cheeky way of saying 'Go home.'

manged – rhymes with banged. Harrassed. 'I'm not going to be messed and manged about like this any longer.'

manky – bad-tempered.

mantling; mantling about – fussing; being actively ineffectual.

man with no hands – measure of miserly habits. 'He gi'es things away like a man with no hands.'

mardy – cross; disagreeable; unco-operative. 'I would have axed her to do it, but she seems a bit mardy this morning.'

Marjorie Moveall – period of brisk activity, especially when repositioning furniture etc. Used when several adjacent houses acquire new occupants in a short space of time.

mary – internal economy; stomach. 'I've got a pain in my mary.'

mash – make tea.

mate – pronounced mairt or mayat; the universal title and form of address for all mankind, friend or foe, high or low, and even husband or wife.

maunge; mange – strictly a skin disease, but used for a less readily defineable ailment: to have the mange means to be mopy, sulky, silently disagreeable. 'Don't ask *her* to play, she's got the maunge.' Maungy, of pets, domestic animals and (facetiously) people means not neat or handsome in appearance. "There's that maungy-looking cat again.'

may – are expected to. 'The more you do, the more you may do.'

meck – make. 'If he thinks he weearn't wock, there's nowt as'll meck him.'

med – made.

medics – remedies, in general of all kinds, but sometimes implying those not prescribed by a physician. Some came from the chemist and were called clats by the cynical; a few were homespun and conjured visions of dark caves and bubbling cauldrons.

meet: 'He'll meet his sen coming back' – comment on the unusually fast rate of somebody's travelling or working.

mending – of the fire in the grate, refuelling. A fire blazing merrily is said to have been mended up nicely. Also, a response to an inquiry into progress after an illness or injury.

messer – dirty, untidy eater.

the mester – the master; one's employer: a respectful term. Occasionally used by a wife of her husband [before Women's Lib!].

mew – mowed. 'I went round and mew all their grass while they was away.'

midden – rubbish-tip.

middling – popular response to 'How are you?' Rarely is exceptionally good health admitted; most conditions range from pretty fair down to a bit poorly, with middling about half way.

midge – mosquito; any smallish flying insect.

milestone inspector – tramp.

mill: 'His mill grinds slow' – he doesn't work very quickly.

millimetre – any very small measurement or distance.

mingy – (the g is soft: as in gentle) stingy; mean; penny-pinching; uncharitable.

mizzle – disappear; go away. Objects of value which disappear and are said to have mizzled have probably, the inference is, been stolen.

mizzling – raining very finely; almost a mist and not quite a drizzle.

mofradite – large waggon with additional sides and ends raised at an outward angle from the customary sides and ends.

moggy – cat. Or a marble. Or a Morris Minor in recent years.

moiling – working feverishly.

mole-skinner – knife. Perhaps originally a particular sort, but applied jocularly to any fearsome-looking knife, and even more jokingly to a very small one. 'Stands theer clearning his finger-nails with his mole-skinner.'

molly – round, straight-side basket used for gathering fruit and other produce. Gooseberry-pickers picked into their own baskets, which they emptied into mollies at the weighing-in point.

money: 'We ain't got much money, but we do see life.' – comment passed when something highly entertaining has been witnessed at no cost.

money spider – Tiny spider which, if allowed to remain on the person, attracts money [or so it is said].

morish; moorish – of food, tasty; making one wish for more.

moulting – (of humans) going bald.

mouth: 'Every time she opens her mouth she puts her foot in it' – she lacks tact.

Moving Day – Lady Day.

mowed out – (mowed rhymes with loud) over-full or stretched. To be mowed out with work is to be fully committed and unable to contract further obligations.

mowing; mowching – (rhymes with sewing) travelling very quickly.

much of a(n) – approximately equal; within the same category. 'That gel o' Jackson's, remember? She's much of an age with our Liz.'

muck – soil. A phrase popular as a conversation-stopper on people who perpetually discuss weather is: 'Aye, and there's a lot o' muck on the ground this year.'

all of a muck sweat – hot and agitated, usually from fear.

mulfry – the 'feel' of the atmosphere during close, thundery weather. Many weather words and phrases, however, get themselves put to inverted use for humorous effect: 'A bit mulfry' might be used on a bitterly cold morning. Two men met in an appalling blizzard, and the greeting was: 'Not many o' them little thunderflies about'.

mun; munt – must; must not. But mun gets used where munt might be expected; it depends on inflexion. 'Yer mun do that, boy,' rising, means 'you must not'.

mush; mushie – mouth, usually of an infant.

muss-tosh – moustache.

N

nag – chew or gnaw, as a dog at a bone.

napper – human head.

napping – habitual rapid blinking of the eyes.

nay – desist. Also, a denial of knowledge: 'Nay, don't ask me', means that I am hardly the person to be able to answer.

nearer: 'The nearer the bone, the sweeter the meat' – a chivalrous defence of ladies who are not too luxuriously upholstered.

nesh – slow to understand, especially of a child.

new land – that recently ploughed from grass.

nice-tish – nice-ish, but generally meaning the opposite of fairly nice. Not a strong condemnation, rather an expression of mild aggrievedness. 'I tried your shop door and it was locked; you're a nice-tish sort of shopkeeper.'

nick – condition. 'It's ten year old, but it's still in good nick.'

nigh on – approaching a given magnitude; very close to but less than. 'There's nigh on fifty ton still in the ground.'

nobby – novel, ingenious, whether useful or not.

noggin – slice or lump, generally of food; a large helping. 'Cut us a good noggin o' that dough-cake.'

nor – than. 'Mablethorpe's further nor what Skeg is.' 'Mine's bigger nor what yourn is.'

nose-warmer – rhymes with boo-as farmer. A clay pipe with its stem broken short, but still in use.

not much about him/her – slow on the uptake; not bright; lacking promise.

November: 'If November ice will bear a duck, the rest of the year'll be slush and muck.'

now then – hello. General greeting, often reduced to 'nairn'.

nunty – small, poky.

O

obstroclous – obstinate; contrary; rebellious.

ode – old.

ode hard – hold hard; wait; before you proceed, heed this.

off – going. 'I'm off to the village when it fines up.' Also of behaviour; a bit off means irregular, unfair, slightly improper but not quite outrageous. Also of foodstuff: sour or fetid.

off-it – travelling very fast. 'Did you see that hare? Goy, it weren't half off-it.'

off-on; off-of – off. 'Tell them kids to get off-on that seed-bed.' 'This was a cutting off-of that one in Mam's garden.'

off to – about to; intending to. In spite of 'off', movement is not necessarily envisaged. 'I'm off to stop here a bit.'

offens – often.

oilskins – waterproof clothing, of whatever material.

old-fashioned – of an infant, apparently perceptive.

old: the old gel – my (or your) mother.

old: the old lady – my mother.

old: the old man (chap) – my (or your) father.

old: my old woman – my wife.

old: my old man – my husband.

old: 'You can't put an old head on young shoulders' – youth has no key to the wisdom of experience.

ommus – almost.

on – of. 'Go round the back on it.'

on the line – employed by the railway company. Also 'on the gas', 'on the 'lectric', 'on the drainage', 'on the post office' – all calculated to be cast-iron jobs-for-life.

One: 'The One Above knows, and He won't split' – an embroidered version of 'God alone knows', meaning 'I don't know, and perhaps nobody does.'

one forrard, two back – 'There was that much ice, every step I took forrard I slipped back two. The onny way I could get here was to tonn round and go back.'

one o'clock half struck – of a person not with it; not keeping pace with current activity; not following the course of events. 'He's like one o'clock half struck.'

one time: at one time – in the past.

'One year's seeds, seven year's weeds' – saying to encourage the use of the hoe: if weeds are left until they drop their seeds, some will still be germinating seven years hence.

onions: their onions – what experts are said to know. 'He was nowt of a player, but when it comes to reffing he knows his onions.'

onion-head – chump; simpleton. Also, a normally reliable person who has had a momentary lapse of concentration.

onion shower – brief rain shower providing just the right amount of moisture for newly-sown onions.

oojah; oojah-kapiff – anything, the name of which is not known or is momentarily forgotten.

opening up – commencing work, especially the act of entering a field to begin harvesting. 'We s'll open up in yon sugar-beet tomorrow.'

operate – rave; express disapproval forcefully; hold forth indignantly. 'Your Dad'll operate when he sees what you've done.'

oppen: 'Every time I oppen my mouth she jumps down my throat' – she disagrees with whatever I say.

orlust – always.

ossacking; hossacking – laughing loudly and coarsely.

ossmuck – horse droppings; stable manure. Applied to (growing) rhubarb and to roses . . . etc. and collected free from the byways, if you got there before the roadman.   '

osso – horse-hoe.

ought; ort – nought; zero; nil. 'O' is seldom spoken to mean zero: 3409 is spoken as 'three, four, ought, nine.'

ounging – rhymes with lounging; repetitive expression of a wish, usually for some material possession. 'That's a coat like the one my wife's been ounging after since back end.'

our kid – my brother or sister, especially if younger than me.

our'n – ours.

outdacious – daring, venturesome.

outs – accomplishment; 'showing' in performance. 'He was always the poorly child, and yet he made more outs than the others.'

outus – outhouse; garden shed; barn; closet.

ower – over; too, when referring to quantity. 'I telled him a score, but he brought one ower many.'

owery – rhymes with showery; wet on the ground, especially when muddy as well.

owt – anything.

P

pad – path. A Southerner who moved to here was puzzled when his new jobbing gardener reported that he had 'wed the pad.' He had weeded the path. The way down the garden is a muck-pad, a gress-pad or an ash-pad, the last frowned on by the housewife because the surface of coal-ash 'treads in'. Meaning that it gets brought back into the house on shoes.

paddling – walking into the house in wet weather, leaving wet foot-marks. 'I wish you'd stop paddling in and out after I've weshed the floor.'

pain in the pluck – feigned illness, suspected of being an avoidance of difficult tasks, situations or weather.

pancheon – large round shallow vessel of earthenware, usually with a dark glaze inside and over the rim.

particular – choosy; fussy; pernickety.

passing bell – church bell tolled on the death of a parishioner, the number of chimes denoting the age of the deceased. For an important departed, a muffled or half-muffled peal might be rung on the day of the funeral.

pawting – pawing the air, in the manner of a cat at play.

peck o' muck – 'Ain't you weshed them radishes afore you're eating them?' 'I rubbed 'em on my sleeve. You got to eat a peck o' muck afore you die!'

peg doll – child's plaything made with an old-fashioned clothes-peg.

pegger – hand tool for making snip-rugs by gripping the snips and drawing them through the harden.

pegging; pegging a rug – the final stage of making a snip-rug. Mam draws the pattern on the harden, sorts the snips into colours and tells where they go. The number of operators depends on the number of peggers available, either owned or borrowed.

peg out – die.

pelting – throwing objects wantonly or mischievously. Also, raining or hailing heavily.

petty – lavatory.

pig cheer – certain perishable edible components (generally offal, or 'pig's fry') traditionally given to friends and neighbours after a killing.

piggle – pick or poke with finger or tool inside an orifice.

piggyback – pickaback; a ride on somebody's back.

pig-poking day – market day, when farmers and butchers walk round the pens before auction time, testing the solidity of the goods (or their tempers) with sticks.

pigs – the word which must not be uttered on any Friday the 13th, though the consequences of doing so are not specified.

pig's fry – see pig cheer.

pig-tates – small potatoes separated by riddling from those destined for human consumption. Being fed to pigs, however, they do ultimately contribute to human contentment.

pincens – pincers; pliers.

'Pinch, punch, the first of the month' – recited for some reason on that particular date and accompanied by the appropriate physical assault on the listener.

pip – to have got the pip is to be out of sorts, in ill humour. An elaboration is 'Got the pip and can't squeak.'

pippin – pipkin; deep earthenware vessel with a lid. We had one for drinking water fetched from the communal pump, one for bread, and a spare one which got filled with delicious herb beer in summer.

pit – open pond; low place, usually wet. Most pits in our village were identified; 'Chantry's pit', the 'vicarage pit', etc.

pittle – urinate; urine.

place – house; domain; farmstead. 'Let's go up to Fred's place a Sunday.'

place names – see 'Cunningsby'.

plasher – hedge-knife.

playing up – behaving badly, especially of children. 'I dooan't know what's gotten into her youngest, allus playing up these days.' Also used of temperamental machinery.

playtime! – addressed to another scholar and accompanied by a display of clenched fist as a warning that, at the time appointed, dreadful things would happen.

plump – exactly; precisely. 'The wind's been plump east all day.'

pocket: in each other's pockets – living closely; having intermingled interests.

poe – chamber-pot. Also called 'the article' or 'the useful article.' An enamelled metal one, being more audible in use, might be called a 'tinklairy'.

poky – small, incommodious; of buildings or rooms therein.

pop – mineral waters; any fizzy drink.

pop-alley – large glass marble, worth two ordinary marbles if plain and three if internally ornamented.

posher – housewife's aid in the weekly wash. An inverted hemispherical (usually copper) bowl with an arrangement of pierced baffles inside and a long wooden handle fixed to the shell. It was used plunger-fashion in the dolly-tub.

posh-rotten – decomposed to softness.

pothook – S-shaped iron hook, engaged in a link of the chain which slid along the potrail above the fireplace, and used to suspend the kettle over the fire.

pot on – 'You've got all your pot on to do that' means that the undertaking contemplated is judged to be at the limit of your capability.

pours: 'It pours and rains' – it is raining fast. Often brings the response: 'Ay, well, if it's doing both I s'll stop in.'

power – pour.

pretty – fairly considerable in size or quantity. 'Pretty big' is bigger than you might have expected, though not enormous. A common reply to an inquiry into one's health is: 'Pretty and well.'

proggle – piggle.

pudding – anything eaten after a main course, whether a pudding or not. It was rumoured that posh people 'sometimes had cheese and biscuits for pudding' Often the pudding was eaten first – said to blunt the appetite for the more expensive meat.

pulk – coward. Usually 'A gret pulk'.

pull – influence, especially in social and worldly affairs. 'He's a useful chap to know; got a lot of pull on the Council.'

pulled – 'He looks as though he's been **pulled** (drawn) through a hedge backards' – comment on unkempt appearance.

pulling – harvesting. Some things are pulled, others picked, cut or lifted. The farmer will say he is lifting potatoes; the people with backache used to say they were picking them. Peas were once pulled at a bob a bag; now they're vined, which is totally mechanical. Strawberries are picked, apples pulled, gooseberries either. Cabbage and cauliflower get cut, brussels sprouts pulled. Beet is lifted. Good luck to them as does it all.

pull up; pull in – stop, as applied to a wheeled vehicle. Pull in implies steering to the side and stopping. Pull up also applies to braking ability: 'I'll have to get the brakes seen to, they don't pull up as they should.' To stop abruptly is to pull up stunt.

the push – the sack; dismissal from office or employment.

puther – pour, rapidly or profusely. 'Rain? It's puthering down!' 'I've never seen so much watter puthering down that dreean.' Also used of smoke, puthering upwards. Of an excessively smoky chimney, 'Somebody's mecking a lot o' puther.'

put it past – 'I wouldn't put it past him (her)' means, 'I can well believe that he (she) would do that.' Always negative.

put on – (first word accented) treated unfairly; generally used when referring to the sharing of work. 'I'm off to see the mester; I weearn't be put on like this.'

putten – put. 'I still ain't found it; it must have got putten somewhere safe.'

put the wood in the hole – shut the door.

Q

quart; quarter – rhyme with cart and carter.

quick – in advance of correct time. 'That clock's ten minutes quick.'

quick hedge – hawthorn hedge.

R

rabbit-meat – lettuce. Also the name is given to dandelion leaves and other delicacies gathered for pet rabbits.

rabbits; white rabbits – what must be said on waking on the first day of the month. The consequences of default are not generally known.

rack your brains – think hard; try to remember something.

rain: does it rain? – form of meteorological enquiry.

rain before seven, fine before eleven (and vice versa) – Unlike most pieces of weather lore, this has one reliable aspect: it rhymes either way.

raining muck-forks, tines downards – raining large spots.

ram-headed – impetuous; reckless. 'Take your time, boy. Dooan't go at it ram-headed'.

ramper – main road. Particular roads are named according to a destination in one direction e.g. 'The Donington Ramper.'

rank – overgrown with weeds.

rare and – added for emphasis. If it: 'Tonned out rare and wet', then it was indeed wet.

rate – right.

rather: 'I'd rather keep him a week than a fotnit' – said of a hearty eater; not in complaint but with admiration and even envy.

rave – express severe disapproval; go on about.

raw – a human physical characteristic meaning lacking in refinement; not merely unkempt, but fundamentally without grace. 'She's a big, raw lass' means that though healthy and even well-proportioned, she is not desirable in the amorous sense. Also of weather, cold.

reach – pass. 'Reach me the salt-pot, will you?'

real – very; considerable. 'I'm not what you'd call real struck on beer.'

reaper file – file made specially for sharpening reaper-blades.

rear – erect; stand on end. 'Fetch yon ladder and rear it agen this stack.'
Also, to raise from birth; used of animals and sometimes plants and
trees.

    – A whimsical, complimentary comment on the obvious good
health of another's child is, 'D'you reckon you'll rear him?'

rearsty; reesty; reested – rotten; smelly; blown; particularly of food-
stuffs.

rec – recreation ground. Ours contained swings, seesaw, bars and a
German field-gun from World War 1 which was melted and returned
at high speed in World War 2.

reckling – as rutlin.

reckon on – anticipate. 'We reckon on being home by midnight.'

reddish – radish.

redler – regular.

reeked; smoke-reeked – smelling of smoke; said of washing which has
been in bonfire smoke. Also, tasting of smoke, as of something
cooked or heated over a smoky fire.

reest – to reest is to lever; to prise something up or apart with a lever.
'Pass us a crowbar; I'll reest it up and put a brick under it.'

rense – rinse. And a light, brief rain-shower. 'I reckon we s'll get a
rense afore the day's out.'

retch – a long road, especially a straight one with few off-turnings.

rhubub – rhubarb.

rick – small stack.

rickback – unsound horse. Also applied half-humorously to the one
man on every farm who can't do particular jobs because of his back.

riddling; tatie riddling – taking potatoes from storage, grading and
bagging them. In the days of graves, this was done in the field,
sometimes using a hessian screen to keep off the lazy winds.

ridging – drawing ridges in the soil ready for seed potatoes to be planted
between them.

rightled; raightled – put right. Both as something which fell and has
been set upright again, and as an injustice remedied. Also, persuaded
to behave properly. Made tidy.

rile – rouse to anger.

ringing the bull – larking about; skiving. From an actual game played
in a barn: a piece of twine hung from a rafter had an iron ring on the

end; it had to be drawn back then swung forward attempting to hook it on to a bull's horn mounted on the wall.

ripsnorter – descriptive of something remarkably big or powerful. 'Watch out for Dennis's bull; he's a ripsnorter!'

rive – split or cut.

road – way; course of action or mode of operation, as well as a defined track. 'Try doing it this road.'

roadman – lengthman; an employee of the County Council, whose job was to keep roads clean with a brush, a shovel, a wheelbarrow, his feet and his muscles. You could see where he had been.

roar – cry, sob.

robbing the barber – letting the hair grow long.

roding – digging and cleaning out the channel of a land-drainage dyke to improve the flow and capacity.

rogue – cultivated plant growing unwanted in a different crop.

roil – disturb a liquid, especially one with odorous solids in it. 'Dooan't go roiling that pond up; stinks bad enough as it is.' Applied also to the human temper.

roped in – recruited. Also completed, accomplished. 'At this rate we shan't get it all roped in afore Christmas.'

rough as soot – inclined to play roughly or boisterously.

round – slice of bread the full size of the loaf.

row of houses – to remind another player that it is but a game, or to minimise to oneself the importance of the outcome, the remark: 'Ah, well, it's not for a row of houses' is passed. The customary response is: 'No, nor yet a gold watch.'

rubbage – rubbish; anything unworthy of consideration. 'Nowt much on telly, onny a load o' rubbage.'

ruckled up – crumpled.

ruckling; ruttling – bronchitic noises, human or animal.

ruckus – ructions.

ructions – fuss; noisy arguments. 'I reckon there'll be ructions at the next meeting.'

rummage – unwanted domestic goods; jumble.

run down – of a person, generally unfit but without an apparent specific disease.

rush – charge, in money. 'How much did they rush you for that marrow?'

rutlin – the weakest or smallest of a litter. Sometimes applied to a member of a human family.

S

sack-tackle – hand-operated hoist in a mill or granary.

salted down – put away safely for future use or consumption.

sanky-doodling – walking slowly and without apparent purpose. 'As if next week'll do.'

sattle – settled. 'We're nicely sattle in our bungalow now.'

sauder – solder.

sauming – singing inexpertly and monotonously.

scallywag – mischievous child.

scar – scare; frighten.

scarring – scaring; crow-scaring; keeping birds off crops.

scene – fuss. 'Calm down, then. Don't make a scene about it.'

scolt – rhymes with halt; scalded.

scope – scoop; utensil for carrying and measuring materials. The tea-scope was kept in the caddy, and tea strength for our pot was decided by the formula: 'Fower scopefuls and a bit, or six if it's Stores tea.'

scrag – give a rough time physically, but with playful rather than aggressive intent. 'If you don't let my toys alon, I s'll scrag you.'

scrag end – unwanted remnant; unharvested part of a crop. 'We'll call them cabbages done; leave the scrag ends for the rabbits.'

scraggy – untidy in appearance.

scranny – distracted. 'A noise like that all the time would drive me scranny.'

scrat – scratch.

scratting; scratting a living – scratching; managing on little; being economical through necessity; existing by farming a small parcel of land. Also, descriptive of work such as harrowing not done effectively.

scrawking – scraping the shoe-toes when walking; of a child, scraping the toes when crawling.

scrawny – of people or animals, thin.

screws, the – rheumatism; any pain resembling that of rheumatism.

scrunch – crunch; the sound of an apple being eaten, or of somebody walking on gravel.

scuffing – loosening the soil between crop rows. Also, footwear or other clothing worn out by unfair usage are said to be scuffed out.

scullery – kitchen. Our living-cum-dining room was always called the kitchen, although the cooking was done in what we called the scullery.

scutch; squtch – stroke of a whip. sound of a stick flicked in the air.

scuttle – domestic coal-bucket.

seedles – seagulls.

see off – force to quit the vicinity or premises. 'See 'em off, boy' is an order to a dog to evict intruders. Also, a person or team soundly defeated in a game have been 'seen off'.

see stars – take a bump on the head.

seg – second participant in a game in which players go in turn. See also fog, lag, and tuzzy-muzzy.

sell the pig! – raise money by some means, however desperate. Not often meant literally; usually a wry commentary on a commonly-experienced financial situation.

selt – sold.

sen – self.

seng – sang. 'It was a lovely evening; the bods seng while after dark.'

senna pods – a herbal remedy for a reluctant bowel.

service, in – working as a domestic servant, usually living in.

set – sat; sitting. 'I've picked nearly two bagfuls while she's been set on that weighing machine.'

set in – of weather, especially rain, likely to continue for some time. Of work, started. 'We s'll get set in ploughing early next week.'

setting – putting plants in the ground. Spring is often called setting time. 'It kep wet raight through till next setting time.' Sometimes also used for seed sowing.

settle – cure. 'Have an aspirin, that'll settle it.'

set-to – with the first word stressed it is a fight, or an argument which promises to become one; whereas to set to is to begin work with a will.

setting in – commencing work: it usually means starting of the work required in a particular field.

set up – of garden, allotment, or market-garden: tilled and sown or planted to its normal capacity. Also, to commence trading: 'He's now set up as a barber.'

seven years bad luck – penalty for breaking a mirror.

shag; black shag – strong tobacco for a pipe. 'Shag it!' said to a dog is an exhortation for it to tear something to pieces.

shan – shy.

sharpish – quickly; willingly.

shavs – shafts of a cart or waggon. The story is often told of a carter who dozed after his midday break and woke to find that his mates had unhitched his horse then put it back in after passing the shavs through a five-barred gate.

shilling – shelling, peas or broad beans.

shimshams for meddlers – busy person's answer to a child's: 'What is that?'

shiver – splinter.

shogging – walking slowly and tiredly.

shoot – organised outing for shooting game or pests. Also, an area of land or a number of fields habitually used or let for shooting.

shot – shirt. 'All right, keep your shot on' means don't lose your temper.

shove-ha'penny – table board game played in pubs, homes, and workplaces.

'Shut the stable door afore the hoss bolts' – fasten your trouser fly.

sifter – short-handled domestic shovel used for coal and general purposes. Often stood in as a dustpan.

siling – raining very fast.

simmerterry – cemetery.

since – ago. 'Not this side o' May Fair, and that was a month since.'

singling – removing plants by hand from thickly-sown rows to leave economical spacing. An unpopular task, now rendered almost unnecessary by improved drilling machinery.

sipe – exude moisture. Cheese which sweats is said to be 'siping a bit.'

six of one and half a dozen of the other – an assessment of the comparitive wickedness of two wrongdoers; a variant of: 'If there's any difference they're both alike.'

sixes and sevens, at – displaying indeterminacy. Of two or more people, perpetually in disagreement.

skee-wiff – misplaced; misaligned. A nose aligned perceptibly east or west on its face is said to be skee-wiff.

skelsh – a very heavy rainfall. 'It come a right skelsh during the night.'

skerrick – very small quantity; residual shred or trace. 'I was hoping for a bit o' that damson pie, but there ain't a skerrick left.'

skerry – horse-drawn tool for loosening soil between rows of growing crops.

skimmer – see hoop and skimmer.

skin: 'You couldn't knock the skin off a rice pudding!' – taunting comment on the fighting prowess of a potential adversary.

skin: the skin of a gnat's eyelash – what a person is said to be 'hanging on by' when in a precarious position physically, financially, or socially.

skin: 'I'll skin you alive' – threat of punishment, seldom enacted.

skirt; skirt-land – agricultural land, the soil of which is neither all peat nor all silt but a mixture of the two.

skivvy – servant, especially a scullery-maid. Also, to do the work of a servant. 'Do it yoursen, I'm not skivvying for you.'

sky-blue-pink (with yellow spots on) – facetious response to an invitation to choose or name a colour.

slack; slacken – slake; quench the thirst. And a blacksmith slacks a piece of iron when he plunges it into his bosh tank to cool it.

slap; slap-bang – accurate; dead-on. 'It flew over their heads and landed slap in the middle of the field.' 'Slap' also means spill: 'Mind you don't slap that juice on the clean cloth.'

slasher – short-bladed hedge-knife; any large knife for outdoor use. Humorously, a very small knife.

slat – flat, thin length of wood used in making fences, boxes, trellis, etc.

slates: a few slates loose – moderately crazy.

slaumy – slow-moving; reluctant; ungainly.

slaver – rhymes with 'have a'; grossly insolent talk. 'I'm not going to listen to any more of your slaver.' Also, to dribble saliva.

slew – swivel; slide or swing across the line of travel.

slipe – path or walkway established by usage rather than design. 'It's a mile round by road, but there's a slipe across yon field.'

slip-side – when a place is adjacent to another but not on the habitual route, it is said to be 'slip-side of it.' 'Quarrington? Aye, it's slip-side o' Sleaford from here.'

slither – sluther; slip.

slive – move or behave surreptitiously. 'Dooan't you slive off afore it finishes, like you did last year.'

slommerky; slummerky – slovenly, of both clothes and manners.

slops – contents of the chamber-pot.

slosh: on the slosh; sloshways; sloshways on – askew; not properly aligned.

sludge – mud.

slurry – thin mud; semi-liquid manure.

sluther – slither; slip; especially on a muddy surface. Also, thin, slippery mud. 'Careful, going across the yard; it's all sluthery.'

smit; smitten – infected, mostly with viral diseases transmitted atmospherically. And meat is smitten when it starts to go rotten. Extended to the imitative acquisition of habits or enthusiasms: 'I never played till I see her playing; it was her as smit me.'

smoking and raining – said of heavy rainfall accompanied by wind.

smother-flies – small, black 'thunder-flies'.

snaffle – pilfer; steal. 'Let's go snaffle some apples off Johnson's.'

snappy – short and sharp in conversational response; peevish.

sneck – gate or door fastener; Suffolk thumb-latch; cabin-hook. And the act of using it: 'Sneck the yard gate as you go out.'

sneck-lifter – Peeping Tom. Implies the habit of gently lifting the sneck of a wash-house door whilst a lady uses her galvanised tub, to peer through the small hole below the lever.

snew – snowed.

snickersneeze – placing thumb and forefinger on either side of another's jawbone and squeezing rhythmically. A playful 'punishment' for a mildly mischievous child. 'I'll snickersneeze you!'

snip-rug – hearth-rug made with snips.

snips – old clothing, etc, cut into short strips for making snip-rugs.

snitch – human nose. A snitchrag is a handkerchief.

snobbing – mending boots and shoes, using a snobbing- or hobbing-iron.

snottynosed lot – family of dirty children.

so by as – so that; in order to. 'Rest the hot end near the point of the anvil, so by as you can hammer it round into an eye.' Facetiously, a 'sobyas' is a gadget or appliance for doing a particular job. 'We should have a sobyas for that, somewhere.'

sock – soak; the level of water saturation below land surface, discovered by digging a hole and waiting for it to rise. 'It's a bad time for grave-digging, with the sock being so high.'

sockrot – drink, with particular reference to that made in a factory.

soft – not very sensible; easily *put* on. A person who 'talks soft' or is 'a bit soft (in the head)' is a long way from insanity but is pointing in that general direction.

sofy – sofa.

sool – attack physically with the object of hurting, though often used playfully in the same sense as 'I'll give you a going-over'. Its most common use is in exhorting a dog to attack: 'Go on, boy; sool him!'

sooner – name given jovially to a dog or cat of unreliable personal habits. 'He'd sooner do it on the doorstep than go down the garden.'

sote – salt.

spadger; spadge – sparrow.

sparrer-gress; sparrow-grass – asparagus.

sparrow's mouthful – unit of measurement for the human appetite. 'Is that all you want? It's not a sparrow's mouthful!' And a poor eater is said to be: 'Not eating enough to keep a sparrow alive.'

spasms, the – bouts of pain or discomfort; usually transient indigestion.

spaw – spa.

speak: 'I speak as I find' – used in discussion of the character of a third party. It means that whatever opinion is held by others, mine is based on my own experience.

speak ill of the dead – something it is said you should never do, thus allowing rogues and scoundrels to become publicly blameless by the simple expedient of dying.

spell; spill – a piece of paper rolled to a convenient shape and size for lighting candles, lamps, and pipes from the fire. A jam-jar inside the fender was kept filled with spells made from pieces of Daily Herald rolled round a knitting-needle.

spifflication – threatened punishment of an unspecified nature. 'If you do that again, you'll be severely spifflicated.'

Spilsby, to go round by – to fall off (a horse or bicycle) on any journey.

spinner; tatie-spinner – implement for raising the potato crop, leaving the tubers on the surface for pickers to collect by hand.

spit – depth in soil equal to the blade length of a spade. 'It's a fairish garden, but it wants digging two spits deep.'

'Spit on it and call it spot' – consolatory phrase used by parents to assure a child that a recently acquired injury is a minor one.

splitting-in – mechanically covering seed potatoes after planting, using an implement which splits the ridge between adjacent rows and deposits the soil over the trenches in which the seeds lie.

spock – spoke; spoken. 'They reckon Bill and his missis hesn't spock for a threwick.'

spotted dick; spotty dick – pudding with visible currants. Also teasingly of a person exhibiting a rash.

spouting – gutters; rainwater furniture in general. Also, talking in an authoritative manner.

spreed – spread. 'No good chucking manure down in heaps, it wants spreeding.'

sprink – sprinkle, especially accidentally.

spud – small hoe, used with a pushing action. Potatoes are seldom called spuds. Another kind of spud is an iron tooth on a tractor wheel, giving tractive grip on soft land.

spuggy – sparrow.

squob-eyed – slanting; not perpendicular. Surfleet is the place with the squob-eyed church.

squad – rhymes with mad; mud.

squits – equals. Called during or after a game or quarrel, when the scores are judged to be level. 'I never hit him very hard, and any road he pulled my hair fost so we're squits.'

squtch – see scutch.

stair-rods – term used to describe heavy, thundery rain.

stalled – replete; unable to eat more, regretfully.

standing; hard standing – patch of hard, dry ground for parking vehicles, implements or crops. A well-appointed farm has ample concrete standings; others, perhaps the rubble from a demolished cottage.

standing water – unwanted flood-water on the land.

stand to – nourish; sustain; satisfy. Said on giving or offering substantial food or drink: 'That'll stand to you, this code weather.'

stanger; butt-stanger – long-handled, pronged implement for catching fish in mud or shallow water. Sometimes shortened to 'stang'.

starnls – starlings.

starving – hungry. Also, cold.

steam: 'I'm not driv by steam!' – I can't work any faster; I'm only human.

steep – soak. Dried peas are steeped overnight for cooking next day.

stemming – walking fast and purposefully. 'I see young Fred stemming away down the back road. Is he off courting?'

stew – hot, steamy atmosphere, especially when accompanied by cooking smells.

stick – tolerate. 'I can't stick that woman at any price.'

sticker – persistent person; trier.

sticking – collecting sticks from hedgerows and trees, to take home for kindling.

stiff – of a situation or proposition, unfair; difficult, even unacceptable. Of a price, high; usually 'a bit stiff'. Of a person, thick-set; not fluent in movements of the limbs.

stilts – the handles of a horse plough.

stitherum – lengthy, complicated, and usually incomprehensible communication. They occur on printed documents such as official forms, and are heard in political speeches, courts of law, and parish council meetings.

stocky – stockdove; wild pigeon.

ston cod – stone cold.

stood – standing. 'He was stood there above an hour, just looking.'

stood off – temporarily suspended from employment, blamelessly; usually through shortage of work.

stop – stay. 'Next holiday, come and stop with us a few days.'

Stores, the – the Co-operative shop.

stowk – (ow as in owl) A number of sheaves of corn stood together for drying. A boy could hide in one.

straddle – measure or gauge the size of a thing with the stride. 'Straddle it out, see what length it is.' Also to stand over something with a foot each side.

strange; strange and – used for emphasis: 'You're strange and quiet.' 'There's a lot of gulls; must be strange and rough at sea.'

stranger – floating tea-leaf, said to predict the arrival of an unknown visitor.

string, on a – being deceived.

strinkle – sprinkle.

struck on – keen about; in favour of; charmed by. Most often negative: 'He's a nice enough feller but I'm not struck on her.' 'We generally wallpaper; I ain't struck on painted walls.'

strut – small fish, common in dykes and drains.

stunt – sudden; abrupt; sharp. Said of movement which changes abruptly: stopping stunt, starting stunt, turning stunt. Also applied to a sharply angular bend in a road or way: 'There's a stunt corner just as you go into the village.'

subsoiling – ploughing deeper than normally.

sucked in – deceived; made the subject of trickery; disappointed.

sugar: neither sugar nor salt – anybody reluctant to go out in the rain, especially to school, was told: 'You're neither sugar nor salt; you'll not melt.'

sup – undefined quantity of liquid. 'Would you try a sup of elderberry wine?' Not necessarily drink, though; 'Been a sup o' rain in the night' might, according to intonation, mean anything from a light shower to a cloudburst.

swap – rhymes with clap. Exchange.

swarm – rhymes with harm. A gathering of insects.

    – also, to climb a pole or trunk by clasping with arms and legs.

sweethearts – 'sticky' seeds of hairiff which cling to fur and clothing.

sweltered – (of a person) uncomfortably hot. 'Leave yon door oppen, I'm sweltered in here.'

swig – brief drink, especially from a bottle. Dad used to take a beer-bottle filled with cold, unsweetened, and unmilked tea to work every day, and take frequent swigs from it.

swill – wash perfunctorily. Also, unappetising food. Pig-swill is kitchen waste or leavings, fed to pigs.

swutch – sound of a stick or whip being wielded. 'He come up with the cows, swutching a bit of willow.' See **scutch**.

syreen – siren.

T

tab – the tongue of leather in a boot, below the lacings.

tackle up – make the necessary preparations before starting a particular job of work.

taffle – tangle; confusion. 'Can you give Dad a hand? He's getting all taffled up with his tax form.'

tainted – jokingly applied to property belonging to an absent party: 'Tain't yours, and 'tain't mine, is it?'

tairts – potatoes [and see tate].

tairtying – harvesting potatoes. Sowing them is 'setting tairts'.

take after – resemble, mostly of offspring said to 'take after' one or the other parent. 'My, he takes after his Dad!'

take on – weep; display misery or consternation. [cf., **took-on** below]

take up – improve. 'We s'll go after dinner if the weather takes up.'

taking in – laundering other people's clothes for hire or reward. Also, providing accommodation for lodgers: 'She teks in, you know.'

'Talk of angels, you hear the flutter of their wings' – said when somebody arrives during a conversation of which they were the subject. A less complimentary version begins: 'Speak of the devil . . .'

talk: making it talk – playing a musical instrument very well.

tap – borrow from a person, especially money. Also, attempt to do so: 'I tapped Dad for some petrol money, but it was no go.'

tases – tastes. 'It tases as though it's been kep near onions.'

tate – potato. Changes to tatie when used adjectivally: tatie merchant; tatie clamp; tatie fork.

tatie – hole in a sock, particularly at the heel, where the protruding wearer resembles a potato.

tatie holiday – additional school holiday to enable children to help in the potato harvest.

tatie-masher – wooden kitchen utensil for mashing cooked potatoes.

tatie-ridger – tool for ridging or hilling for the potato crop.

tatie-trap – human mouth.

tea – meal taken after the day's work, in late afternoon or early evening. Whatever its size and form it is still tea, never dinner.

tea-tin – white enamelled tin with blue beaded edges, tapered inward from bottom to top, fitted with loose lid and top carrying handle made to swivel. Used to take tea from farmhouse kitchen to field.

teeming – pouring liquid from a vessel. Also, raining fast. 'Let's hang on a bit, it's teeming down.'

tecking, in a – in a taking; in a state of distress or agitation. 'I couldn't meck no sense on him; he was still in a tecking ower losing his pigs.'

tem – teemed; poured. 'I've tem you another cup.'

tensy – child's solitary ball game, requiring a high blank wall and a good bouncer.

tenting – minding; watching and controlling the movements of grazing animals, especially those put out on roadside verges. 'I used to earn a penny a day, tenting cows.'

tep – tipped. 'He driv his tractor to, gain o' the dyke and tep it ower.'

terror; little terror – unruly person or child.

tewed – harrowed; very tired, especially when short of breath. 'Dooan't do too much and tew your sen.'

thack – thatch. 'Stacking and thacking' is the art of making stacks which laugh at weather.

that – of course; emphatically. 'Poison you? That it weearn't!'

theirn – theirs.

then – than. 'She's younger then what I am.'

'There and back to see how far it is.' – evasive answer to the question: 'Where have you been?'

thew – thawed. 'It thew all afternoon in the sun.'

thick – of personal relationships; close; very friendly. Sometimes mildly sinister: 'Them two's getting thick; I wonder what they're up to.'

thick end – larger quantity; majority. 'There's the thick end of a lorry-load in the other field.'

thin – of weather, cold; bleak.

thing-a-poppus – thing on purpose. Something made specially for the job, the proper name of which is not known, is temporarily forgotten, or is irrelevant. 'You'll not get that pulley off wi'out a thing-a-poppus to draw it.' See also 'so by as'.

things – see **threes** below.

thinks nowt on – thinks nothing of; finds it easy. 'He reads a book in a day, thinks nowt on it.'

thon; thonder – yon; yonder. With a soft th, as in then.

thow – rhymes with snow; thaw.

three parts – three quarters.

threes: 'Things happen in threes' – calamities come in cycles of three. On breaking a dish, a housewife might say: 'There! I got a puncture this morning and now this, so there's another to come.'

threshing set – a full set on the road was: steam traction engine, drum, jack, and living-van. In season, two of our neighbours left at five on a Monday morning to light the fires, travelled the farms threshing through the week, and returned in time for Saturday dinner.

threwick – period of time, equal to seven days longer than a fotnit.

thribble; threbble – treble, meaning threefold but not an unbroken choirboy's voice.

throng – busy; energetically occupied. Sometimes 'fine and throng' or even 'strange and throng'.

thruff – through.

thunderbox – lavatory, especially the square wooden box style.

ticket: 'That's the ticket!' – that is satisfactory.

tide-mark – boundary of washed area on a child's face, as detected by an eagle-eyed mother.

tide-mist – light coastal mist, said to come and go with the tide.

tidy – considerable. 'A tidy few' is not a smaller number than expected, but a larger. 'Quite a tidy place' means a large place, and still applies if it's a shambles.

tidy-betty – heavy, ornamented cast-iron screen standing in the hearth immediately below the grate, enclosing the space into which ashes fall. It is as black as a fenland night but more cheerful, being polished to a shine every Saturday morning with a brush and some Zebo Grate Polish.

tiggy – another name for the game of tag, or 'its'.

tight 'un, a – as well as the miserly connotation, this means 'a character', somebody who can be expected to do the unexpected or outrageous.

tilly-willy – ineffectual; cheap and nasty. Applied to things too small, weak or badly fashioned to do their intended job.

tincher – tincture; a very small measure or quantity.

tinklairy – barrel-organ. A man used to come round house-to-house carrying one by a shoulder-strap; it had a single leg to stand it on for the concert. It played *most* of 'The Stars and Stripes' march, the omissions being irregularly spaced throughout. [and see poe]

tinpot Caesar – person of self-exaggerated importance. 'Take no notice of him, he's a bit of a tinpot Caesar.'

tipple – tip or pour. 'Tipple all them berries into one bowl.'

titivate – superficially improve in appearance.

tittle – tickle.

Tommy Lidgett – a clock or watch. Refers to an itinerant vendor of them who conducted auctions at village inns, etc in the last century. 'Now, what's the time by your Tommy Lidgett?'

tonned – turned.

took on – engaged in employment. The process of becoming employed is 'getting took on', and an employer wishing to recruit is said to be 'taking on'. The opposite processes are 'laid off' or 'stood off'.

tooling – processing arable land mechanically with tractors, ploughs, harrows, rolls, etc. Applied mainly to texturing operations, seldom to sowing or harvesting.

top coat – homespun meteorological term meaning a difference of temperature, usually measuring present coldness against past warmth. 'Damn this eerst wind! It's a top coat colder'n it was yisty!'

topping – removing leaves of a root-crop. Topping and tailing, however, is preparing gooseberries by removing the stalk and flower. A popular joke refers to mythical employment as a gooseberry shaver, who also removes the whiskers and sells them as grapes.

tosh – moustache.

touched – daft. 'The way she goes on, I reckon she's a bit touched.'

toucher – a close-run thing; a near-miss. 'He did just clear the gairt-post, near as a toucher.'

trains: 'Go and play trains' – go away; don't bother me.

traipse – walk wearily, especially in fruitless quest of something. 'All afternoon we was, traipsing round that blessed market.'

tramming – travelling fast.

tram-smash – standard of facial beauty. 'She's got a face like the back end of a tram-smash.'

treat – organised party or outing for children. We had a Buff's treat and a Chapel Sunday School treat every year.

tret – treated. 'The mester took us down to the Bull and tret us.'

tripe waiting for vinegar/onions – descriptive of somebody inactive amid activity, or taking a long time to consider a matter. Also a piece of work abandoned, being complete except for a minor omission.

trots, the – frequent bowel action; diarrhoea.

trud – trod. 'He's trud on my engine and bosted it!'

trup – tripped. 'I trup ower the mat as I come in.'

'That's the tune the cat died on' – critical comment on a musical performance.

Turk; young Turk – mischievous or precocious child or young person.

turned round – having finished all expected or scheduled work 'We've just about got the harvest turned round.' Also of the passage of time: 'Get this month turned round, we s'll be a bit easier.'

turned over – of the land, dug or ploughed. 'I try and get it all tonned ower afore back end.'

tushies; tushy-pegs – infants' teeth.

tuts – belongings in a portable state. 'Pick up your tuts and let's be off.'

tuzzy-muzzy – deliberate theft performed openly, especially of marbles.

twang – alien manner of speech, e.g. Yorkshire twang, American twang.

twank – chastise, usually by smacking.

twig – click; suddenly understand. 'It took me a minute afore I twigged what he meant.'

twitch – coarse grass with white, stringy root. Thrives in neglected gardens. An indifferent gardener might be asked, 'How's the twitch-beds coming on?' The distinctive smell of burning twitch gives rise to the chaffing suffered by pipe-smokers who light up in company: 'Hello! Somebody bonning twitch?'

twizzened – twisted. 'Hold on a bit; the rope's gotten all twizzened.' Anything 'twizzened and jorped' is indeed in a state.

twizzle – spin.

two-penn'orth: 'Like two-penn'orth of death warmed up' – looking poorly; lacking drive and energy.

U

undernean – underneath.

uneppen; unheppen – clumsy; not very clever with the hands. Applied to both habitual and transient clumsiness. 'That's another you've dropped; you're strange and uneppen tonight.'

union – workhouse.

up below – warning shouted by a worker above, that something is to be lowered or dropped.

unput – unfastened, of something intended to be permanently fastened. 'This coat's ewsless; all the seams is coming unput.'

up the wooden hill (to Bedfordshire) – to bed.

uppity – affecting superiority. 'I wouldn't ask him, he seems a bit uppity these days.'

urrrr – pronounced gutturally, yes. Or, on occasions, no. On a rising note it means eh?

us – me. 'Get us a drink, mate.'

utching – moving along by the bottom, feet and hands, as a child. see bumming.

utch-up – move along (seat or form) to make room.

V

vally – value.

vingidder – vinegar.

W

wack – payment due, particularly for services rendered.

wacken – waken; wake. 'I dooan't need a lurrum, I can wacken any time I want.' A dreamy or reluctant worker might be urged: 'Wacken yoursen up!'

waddle – rhymes with addle; walk with lateral oscillation, like a duck.

wang – throw forcibly, as in wellie-wanging competitions.

want – rhymes with pant; ought. 'You want to do it properly', means that you ought to do it properly.

war – was. 'He said the second house down the drove, but there war only the one.'

ware – potatoes which stay in the riddle, suitable for human consumption.

warm – rhymes with harm, especially when referring to chastisement: 'I'll warm your hide if you don't geower.'

wars: in the wars – injured. Of somebody wearing even a small bandage: 'I see he's been in the wars.'

wash-hand stand – a piece of bedroom furniture: a wooden stand, the posh ones marble-topped, with a hole to take a basin, and a matching jug and soap-dish.

wassing – rhymes with passing; usually 'wassing in' or 'wassing in at'. It means working energetically. 'If the weather holds, we shall be wassing in at the planting all this week.'

water bewitched – weak tea.

watter-hen – water-hen; moor-hen.

way on – district; direction. 'He lives Wrangle way on' means somewhere vaguely in that area. 'After we left Spalding, we went Bourne way on for a bit.'

wear and tear -- both rhyme with beer: so does swear.

weather-breeder – a day of weather which is ominously good, at a time when the opposite was expected.

weearn't; wooan't; wairn't; wain't; – all mean won't or will not. 'You try telling her; she weearn't do nowt as I say.'

wed – weeded. 'We wed nearly an acre of onions.'

well away; well off – soundly asleep.

'We'll have two o' them' – facetious response when something outrageously expensive has been described.

wellie – pressure on the accelerator pedal of a driven vehicle. 'Give it some wellie!' is an exhortation for more speed or power.

welt – strike, especially with a whip or belt.

wesh – wash.

weshus – washhouse; the outhouse containing the copper, copper-stick, mangle, dolly-tub, dolly or posher, clothes-basket and peg-bag. Sometimes also a washboard, a wooden box for the Sunlight soap, a Reckitt's Blue Bag and some Colman's starch.

Wesleyan hammer – one with two faces.

wet and warm – description of a 'hot' beverage, meaning acceptable; palatable; not brilliant but welcome anyway.

wet time – that during which, due to rain, work is unable to proceed outdoors. Land workers were said to 'lose wet time' if their pay stopped.

'What's the clock say?' – What time is it? A lad proudly wearing a watch-chain for the first time could expect to be asked: 'What's the time by your watch and chain?'

wheelbarrow – word used as a substitute, when reading aloud, for any long word which is difficult to pronounce.

wheel: 'We had one but the wheel come off' – stock response of a person who has been told the proper (but unfamiliar) name of some new-fangled apparatus.

when he's at home – at mention of an unfamiliar personal name, somebody might ask, 'Who's he when he's at home?' It means: 'Where's he from, what does he do, how does he fit into your story?'

'When the sun shines both sides the hedges' – equal to 'when pigs fly'. It means 'never'. 'Mam, when can I have a bike?' was a good way to evoke this response.

while – till, until. 'Not now; you'll have to wait while Friday.'

whistle – bottle; hum; smell strongly.

whistler – potato with a deep slug-hole, which may produce a musical note if held up in a strong wind. At the tatie-grave during riddling, the foreman might say, 'Chuck any whistlers out.'

whistle wockit! – we shall work it! Take heart, lads—we're winning!

whoa, Emma, set your foot – stop! wait! Said also to one already stopped but showing signs of moving. Also to a talker who has overlooked something important.

wick – mechanical power; potential power. A powerful car or motorcycle was said to have 'plenty of wick'. Early wick-operated carburettors would deliver more fuel in response to 'tonning the wick up', the phrase carrying over into the days of the butterfly throttle.

Will's tairts – a common remark on the possibility of forthcoming foul weather, based on observation of a nearby rain-cloud, is 'It looks a bit black ower Will's tairts.'

wim-wams (for window-shutters); ditto (for shoeing ducks) – see shim-shams for meddlers.

windling – winnowing; cleaning seed in the wind.

winder-brecker – window breaker; outdoor spinning top, used with a whip, having a mushroom shape and the ability under a skilled hand to leap up to window height and land again still spinning.

wire – telegram.

wittle; witter – complain or agitate continuously. 'There's nowt as can be done about it, so geower wittling.'

wocked up – worked up; having completed all the work expected of one.

woe; woo – stop. Odd that, in a county renowned for double vowel sounds, the word commonly spelt 'whoa' is pronounced with a single vowel sound. Originally addressed only to horses, its use has extended to all activities.

woms – earthworms.

wonderful – considerable; gives emphasis to quality or magnitude, but often negatively. 'I've seen his best marrows, and they ain't so wonderful big.'

wonky – not functioning properly.

wonser – heavy blow, sufficient alone (once-er?) to conclude a fight.

wood coat – coffin.

work – do, or accomplish. 'You have a go if you think you can work it.'

working; making work – showing signs of beginning to ferment.

wost – worst. 'I don't know which is wost, being busy or trying to look busy.'

woth – worth. 'What's it woth to keep my tatie-trap shut?'

wowser – moustache, especially a luxuriant one.

Wragby way on – 'You look as though you're going Wragby way on.' means that your clothes are worn or torn. Also applied to otherwise faultless apparel which has suffered accidental damage.

wrap yoursen around this – eat (or drink) this.

wristwatch – 'talking wristwatch' is using pronunciation normally associated with a wealthier stratum of society.

wun – wound, as in reference to a spring. 'Hes yon clock been wun up?'

wurry; wurrit – worry. And a wurryguts is somebody habitually doing so.

—-oOOo—-

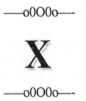

X

—-oOOo—-

Y

yard-brush – stiff-bristled sweeping brush.

yard of pump water, a – what a thin person, especially if tall and of little interest to a sculptor, is said to resemble.

yawping – singing loudly in a high voice.

yer – expression of disbelief or scepticism, equivalent to the cynical 'Sez you' or 'Oh yeah?'

yest – yeast. Baker's yest was taken medicinally, 'to purify the blood.'

yit; yet – still; even to this time. 'He went to see the gaffer about it, and for owt I know he's there yit.' Slightly exclamatory, as if he wasn't expected to be there so long.

yisty – yesterday. A yisty's loaf is one baked yesterday.

yock – yoke; the formed wooden apparatus fitting across the shoulders which enables the agricultural worker to carry two buckets of water and light his pipe simultaneously.

yocked; yocked on – fastened or 'yoked' for pulling. 'Let's get the van yocked on and we'll be away.'

yonaways – in the direction indicated.

yoo-ee! – call to draw attention, similar to coo-ee.

young 'un; younkster – child.

your eye o' you – scolding phrase, delivered in a threatening growl and seldom used facetiously.

yourn – yours.

yuck – pull sharply, with jerking motion. Also used of a heavy towing operation: 'Hed the tractor down the dyke, but Jim fetched the crawler and yucked it out.'

——oOOo——

——oOOo——